The
GEMINI
Path

YOUR DAILY 2026 HOROSCOPE GUIDE

AMANDA M CLARKE

Copyright © Amanda M Clarke 2026
KORU Publishing

All rights reserved. All content, materials, and intellectual property in this book or any other platform owned by Koru Publishing are protected by copyright laws. This includes text, images, graphics, videos, audio, software, and any other form of content that may be produced by Koru Publishing.

No part of this content may be reproduced, distributed, or transmitted in any form or by any means without the prior written permission of Koru Publishing. This means that you cannot copy, reproduce, or use any of the content in this book for commercial or personal purposes without the express written consent of Koru Publishing.

Unauthorized use of any copyrighted material owned by Koru Publishing may result in legal action being taken against you. Koru Publishing reserves the right to pursue all available legal remedies against any individual or entity found to be infringing on its copyright.

In summary, Koru Publishing © 2024 holds exclusive rights to all the content produced by it, and any unauthorized use of such content will result in legal action.

KORU Publishing

KORU (Maori;NZ)
A symbol of spiritual growth and spiritual connection.

Rocky Point Townhouse, CHRISTMAS ISLAND, Western Australia 6798

ISBN: 978-1-923614-07-9

More on the Bookshelves at
www.theliteraryoracle.com

Disclaimer: The Gemini Path: Your daily 2026 horoscope guide book provides information on astrological readings and intuitive interpretations, it is not intended as a substitute for professional advice, diagnosis, or treatment. The information contained in this book is provided for educational and entertainment purposes only and is not meant to be taken as specific advice for individual circumstances. The author and publisher make no representations or warranties with respect to the accuracy or completeness of the contents of this book and specifically disclaim any implied warranties of merchantability or fitness for a particular purpose. The reader should always consult with a licensed professional for any specific concerns or questions. The author and publisher shall not be liable for any loss or damage caused or alleged to have been caused, directly or indirectly, by the information contained in this book. The use of this book is at the reader's sole risk

More from Amanda Clarke
The Literary Oracle
www.theliteracyoracle.com

The "Daily Guidance" series offers an innovative approach to finding spiritual wisdom and practical advice. Each book in the series is a unique tool designed for daily introspection and decision-making. Readers are invited to meditate on a question or seek general guidance for the day, then flip to a random page in the book. The page they land on provides a personalized message from various spiritual sources, such as angels, tarot, or spirit animals. With each turn of the page, these books deliver insightful, positive messages and mantras to inspire personal growth and provide clarity on life's daily challenges and decisions.

Other books in this series:-
The Angelic Oracles
Daily Angel Tarot Reading
Mystic Tarot Cat
Oracle of the Tarot Cat
Vibes Unveiled
Spirit Animal Oracle
Answers from the Oracles
Messages from the Angels

Daily Guidance
SERIES

Supporting Indie Authors

Love your daily guidance? You can grab more of my books direct from The Literary Oracle: www.theliteraryoracle.com

Buying direct means:
- Much better prices for you + free shipping.
- More support for me as an indie author
- More magical books in your hands

My books are also available worldwide through online bookstores, but direct purchases help keep the magic flowing.

Thank you for supporting indie creativity!

Scan me

Welcome to The Gemini Path: Your Daily 2026 Horoscope Guide — your lively, thought-provoking companion for the year ahead. Crafted for the curious, adaptable, and quick-witted Gemini, this guide honours the way you move through life — with restless energy, sharp ideas, and a heart that seeks both freedom and connection.

Inside, you'll find daily horoscopes paired with affirmations designed to flow in harmony with your natural strengths. Each reading is here to help you navigate 2026 with awareness — whether you're pursuing fresh adventures, deepening relationships, exploring new ideas, or simply learning when to pause and listen to your inner voice.

This isn't about scattering yourself in all directions, it's about balance. As you turn each page, you'll gather clarity, encouragement, and cosmic nudges to focus your energy where it matters most. Let this be the year you embrace your dual nature fully — celebrating your playful curiosity while grounding yourself in choices that align with your truth.

The Answers You Seek

Are Within

January 2026

Gemini
01-January-2026

Gemini, you're stepping into the new year with Mercury lighting up your intentions. Your curiosity and adaptable nature are your greatest strengths today. Conversations flow easily, and the right words will seem to appear when you need them most. Don't be surprised if an old friend reaches out or a message sparks a new idea. This is a good day to set your tone for 2026 with mental clarity. Write your goals down, but keep them flexible—you thrive when you leave room for the unexpected.

Affirmation & Gratitude

"I welcome the new year with curiosity, openness, and the courage to explore life's unfolding opportunities."

Gemini
02-January-2026

The Moon energises your social sector, Gemini, urging you to connect with people who make your spirit light up. You may feel pulled in multiple directions, but your adaptability will allow you to handle it all. A chance meeting or online exchange could lead to something valuable, whether friendship, collaboration, or romance. Be mindful not to overcommit yourself too early in the year. It's okay to say no when needed. Focus on quality interactions rather than quantity.

Affirmation & Gratitude

"I am grateful for connections that uplift me and for the wisdom to know when to say no."

Gemini
03-January-2026

Today, Gemini, your mind is buzzing with ideas, but Mercury's position encourages you to ground those thoughts. If you scatter your energy, you may feel drained or frustrated. Instead, pick one project or idea and devote your time to it. Conversations may veer into deeper, more meaningful territory—don't shy away. You have the gift of translating complexity into simple truths, and people will appreciate your perspective. Journaling will be particularly powerful now.

Affirmation & Gratitude

"I give my energy to what matters most and trust that my ideas will take shape in the right time."

Gemini
04-January-2026

The cosmic energy brings focus to your home and personal life today. You may feel the need to slow down and recharge. Tidy spaces, light candles, or cook a nourishing meal—these small rituals can ground your quicksilver nature. Family or household matters could surface; approach them with patience rather than rushing through. This is also a good day to reaffirm your sense of safety and belonging. Your inner world matters just as much as the outer.

Affirmation & Gratitude

"I honour the sanctuary of my home and the peace it brings to my heart and mind."

Gemini
05-January-2026

Gemini, today emphasises your career and ambitions. You may feel the universe nudging you to speak up or showcase your talents. Don't hold back—your natural charm and wit will work in your favour. A mentor, boss, or colleague may notice your efforts, so step confidently into the spotlight. Be cautious of spreading yourself thin with too many commitments. Choose what aligns most with your long-term goals.

Affirmation & Gratitude

"I am grateful for my unique skills and the recognition that flows when I share them with authenticity."

Gemini
06-January-2026

The Moon's influence today highlights your need for balance between logic and emotion. You may find yourself overthinking or analysing situations that require you to simply feel. Take time for quiet reflection, or let creativity guide you. Music, art, or even a walk in nature could bring the clarity you're searching for. Avoid overloading yourself with tasks. You shine brightest when you give yourself room to breathe and process.

Affirmation & Gratitude

"I trust the balance of my mind and heart, knowing each has wisdom to guide me forward."

Gemini
07-January-2026

Communication is the theme of the day, Gemini. Expect plenty of emails, calls, or conversations. Some may be trivial, but one in particular could prove pivotal. Listen carefully—between the lines lies the message you need. Your humour and quick wit make you magnetic, but remember that listening is as powerful as speaking. If a misunderstanding arises, clear it up quickly. People value your honesty when it's paired with kindness.

Affirmation & Gratitude

"I am thankful for the gift of communication and the way it strengthens my bonds with others."

Gemini
03-January-2026

Gemini, today's cosmic flow has you buzzing with creative energy, but it may feel scattered if you don't anchor it. You'll find inspiration in conversations, books, or even scrolling online, but be mindful not to drift into endless distractions. Focus on weaving one of those sparks into something tangible. Your adaptability makes you brilliant at multitasking, yet sometimes the most growth happens when you commit to just one idea. Trust your instincts, but also give yourself space to review details before rushing. A little discipline today will yield a big payoff tomorrow.

Affirmation & Gratitude

"I channel my creativity into focused action, trusting that what I start today will grow into something meaningful."

Gemini
09-January-2026

The Moon illuminates your partnerships, bringing attention to how you balance giving and receiving in relationships. Whether in love, friendship, or business, you may notice where the scales tip too far one way. Use your natural communication skills to speak your truth with clarity. This isn't about keeping score but about ensuring harmony and fairness. If tension arises, don't shy away—it's an opportunity to strengthen the connection. When you listen as openly as you speak, you'll discover deeper understanding and mutual respect.

Affirmation & Gratitude

"I am grateful for the relationships that mirror growth, balance, and genuine connection in my life."

Gemini
10-January-2026

Today is a day of introspection, Gemini. The universe is nudging you to step back from the noise and check in with your inner self. You may feel more reflective, craving quiet moments away from your usual chatter-filled rhythm. Meditation, journaling, or even a slow walk can help you connect with your deeper needs. Trust that it's okay to retreat—this is where clarity is born. Hidden insights may surface, reminding you that not everything needs immediate answers. Allow stillness to guide your next move.

Affirmation & Gratitude

"I value moments of silence, knowing they reveal the wisdom I need for my journey."

Gemini
11-January-2026

A burst of energy surrounds your work and daily routines today, Gemini. You may feel the urge to organise, declutter, or refine how you manage your time. Pay attention to small details—they could make a big difference in your efficiency and peace of mind. If health matters arise, this is a reminder to care for your body as diligently as you care for your mind. The universe is supporting steady progress now, so take consistent steps rather than chasing quick wins. Practical effort today builds future stability.

Affirmation & Gratitude

"I am grateful for my energy, focus, and the progress I create through steady, mindful actions."

Gemini
12-January-2026

Your playful, adventurous side is calling, Gemini. The stars encourage you to explore something outside your usual routine—whether through travel, learning, or simply trying a new experience. Conversations with people from different backgrounds may open your mind to fresh perspectives. You thrive on variety, and today is perfect for stretching your boundaries. Don't fear the unknown; see it as a chance to expand your horizons. Your curiosity is your compass, and it will guide you toward exciting discoveries.

Affirmation & Gratitude

"I embrace new experiences with curiosity, knowing each step outside my comfort zone expands my world."

Gemini
13-January-2026

The cosmos spotlights your career and reputation today. Recognition for your skills or ideas may arrive, and it's time to own your brilliance. You're often the one who lightens the mood or sparks fresh solutions, but today, you're also seen as a leader. Step into this role without hesitation—your confidence inspires others. Be mindful not to overpromise; it's your consistency, not just your charm, that leaves a lasting impact. The seeds you plant now will shape your future direction.

Affirmation & Gratitude

"I am thankful for the opportunities to share my talents and the confidence to lead with integrity."

Gemini
14-January-2026

The energy shifts inward again today, Gemini, reminding you to check the balance between your outer ambitions and inner world. You may crave solitude or find yourself daydreaming about deeper purpose. Spiritual practices, creative outlets, or time with close loved ones will soothe you. Don't dismiss these softer needs—they are just as vital as your social and professional roles. Trust that pausing and reflecting today will recharge you for the weeks ahead. The universe is whispering through your intuition—be still and listen.

Affirmation & Gratitude

"I honour my inner voice and allow space for reflection, knowing it guides me toward truth and balance."

Gemini

15-January-2026

Gemini, today highlights friendships and group connections. You may find yourself drawn into community activities or collaborating with like-minded people. Your natural gift for communication makes you the spark that keeps the energy alive. Pay attention to new people entering your circle—they could bring opportunities or ideas that align with your long-term vision. At the same time, be mindful not to spread yourself too thin trying to please everyone. Honour your role as a connector while staying true to your own values. Your influence today can inspire unity and progress.

Affirmation & Gratitude

"I am grateful for the friendships and communities that support my growth and inspire my dreams."

Gemini
16-January-2026

The cosmos turns your attention inward, Gemini, urging you to retreat and recharge. After days of buzzing energy, today calls for quiet reflection. Pay attention to your dreams or intuitive nudges; hidden insights are trying to reach you. Journaling or meditation will help you untangle complex thoughts and reconnect with your inner compass. This is not a day for rushing or forcing outcomes—rest is productive when it restores your clarity. Let go of the need to always be 'on' and allow yourself to pause.

Affirmation & Gratitude

"I honour my need for rest, trusting that stillness brings clarity and renewal to my spirit."

Gemini

17-January-2026

Today shines a spotlight on your self-expression and confidence. Gemini, you may feel a surge of courage to speak your truth or showcase your talents. Opportunities to present, perform, or simply share your ideas are supported by the stars. Don't let self-doubt creep in—you've earned the recognition that's coming your way. Your words carry weight, and your ability to articulate complex ideas in simple ways will win others over. Stand tall and let your brilliance shine unapologetically.

Affirmation & Gratitude

"I am thankful for my voice and the courage to share my gifts with the world."

Gemini

18-January-2026

Relationships take centre stage today, Gemini. Whether romantic, professional, or platonic, you'll be asked to evaluate balance and fairness within your partnerships. It's a good day to clear the air, address misunderstandings, or reaffirm commitments. Your natural charm can smooth over rough edges, but remember that honesty is essential. Don't sugar-coat what needs to be said. When you communicate openly and listen in return, you create stronger, more authentic bonds that can carry you forward.

Affirmation & Gratitude

"I appreciate the harmony in my relationships and the honesty that deepens genuine connection."

Gemini
19-January-2026

Practical matters rise to the surface, Gemini. You may need to handle finances, health routines, or organisational details that you've been putting off. Though not always your favourite focus, taking care of these tasks will free up mental energy. The stars encourage you to approach them with steady determination rather than your usual quick fix. Small, consistent steps will build into long-term stability. Don't be discouraged if progress feels slow—this is how you lay foundations for future success.

Affirmation & Gratitude

"I am grateful for the structure and discipline that support my long-term wellbeing and success."

Gemini
20-January-2026

Adventure is calling, Gemini, and the stars push you to stretch beyond the familiar. This could show up as travel plans, exploring new cultures, or diving into a subject that expands your worldview. Conversations with people from different backgrounds will spark inspiration and broaden your perspective. You thrive when you're learning and exploring, and today is a reminder that your mind is your greatest passport. Say yes to opportunities that excite your curiosity—they will open unexpected doors.

Affirmation & Gratitude

"I welcome new adventures and learning, knowing each experience enriches my perspective and nourishes my spirit."

Gemini
21-January-2026

Your career and public image come into focus today, Gemini. Recognition for your work may arrive, or you may feel pushed into the spotlight. Don't shy away—this is the universe's way of affirming your efforts. Step forward with confidence, but remember that authenticity is more powerful than perfection. A mentor or authority figure could offer advice, so listen closely. This is also a good time to reflect on your long-term goals and ensure your actions align with them.

Affirmation & Gratitude

"I am grateful for the recognition of my efforts and the clarity that guides my professional path."

Gemini
22-January-2026

Gemini, today's cosmic focus is on friendships and group activities. You may feel inspired to collaborate on a shared vision or lend your voice to a cause close to your heart. Your ability to communicate ideas clearly makes you a natural leader in these settings. However, be cautious not to get swept into group drama or distracted by competing opinions. Stand firm in your values while remaining open-minded. Networking now could lead to opportunities that align with your long-term dreams, so stay alert to who crosses your path.

Affirmation & Gratitude

"I value the connections that bring purpose and joy into my life, knowing we rise higher together."

Gemini

23-January-2026

Intuition runs strong today, Gemini. You may notice signs, dreams, or subtle nudges guiding your decisions. Don't dismiss them as coincidence—your inner compass is especially accurate now. This is a day for trusting gut feelings rather than overthinking. Spend time in solitude if possible; reflection will reveal answers you've been searching for. Your natural curiosity may tempt you to seek external advice, but the wisdom lies within. Honour that voice, and you'll feel a deeper sense of alignment.

Affirmation & Gratitude

"I trust my intuition to lead me toward truth and decisions that honour my highest good."

Gemini
24-January-2026

Energy shifts toward your individuality, Gemini, giving you the confidence to stand out. You may feel drawn to showcase your talents, speak up in meetings, or embrace a leadership role. This isn't about ego but about stepping into your natural brilliance. Others are noticing your charm, wit, and ideas, so allow yourself to shine without apology. If doubts creep in, remind yourself that you've worked hard for these moments of recognition. Be bold—the universe is backing you.

Affirmation & Gratitude

"I am grateful for my courage to step forward and the light I share with others."

Gemini

25-January-2026

Relationships take centre stage again, and you may need to navigate compromise and collaboration. Gemini, you thrive on communication, and today your ability to bridge gaps will be invaluable. A partner may need reassurance, or a close friend might seek your perspective. Be present and listen as much as you speak. Any tension can be resolved with patience and honesty. This day reminds you that strong partnerships are built not only on fun but also on mutual effort and trust.

Affirmation & Gratitude

"I appreciate the balance and trust that make my relationships meaningful and strong."

Gemini
26-January-2026

Today highlights the practical side of life, Gemini. You may find yourself dealing with finances, work routines, or health matters that require attention. While these tasks may feel mundane, they're essential for maintaining balance. Take a structured approach rather than bouncing between tasks—your energy will feel steadier that way. If health issues have been on your mind, this is a good day to implement small but lasting changes. Think of today as building bricks in the foundation of your future stability.

Affirmation & Gratitude

"I am thankful for the discipline and care that keep my life steady and secure."

Gemini

27-January-2026

Your adventurous side is awakened today, Gemini. The stars encourage you to step out of your comfort zone and pursue experiences that inspire growth. This could mean travel, learning, or simply saying yes to something new. Your curiosity is a gift, and when you follow it, you discover opportunities others overlook. Don't let fear of the unknown hold you back—this is a time for exploration. Even small shifts in perspective can open doors to exciting possibilities.

Affirmation & Gratitude

"I welcome new experiences with an open heart, knowing they expand my horizons and enrich my life."

Gemini

28-January-2026

The cosmos shines a spotlight on your professional life and long-term ambitions today. Recognition for your work is possible, or you may feel a strong push to clarify your career goals. This is a day to be strategic, Gemini—think about where you're heading and how to align your daily actions with your bigger vision. A mentor or authority figure could play an important role, offering guidance or opening doors. Stand tall and own your path with confidence.

Affirmation & Gratitude

"I am grateful for clarity in my ambitions and for the opportunities that guide me toward success."

Gemini
29-January-2026

Gemini, today invites you to pause and reflect on your deeper motivations. You may feel less interested in social buzz and more inclined to explore what's happening beneath the surface. This is a powerful time for self-discovery, so don't shy away from asking yourself the bigger questions: What drives me? What do I truly value? If emotions rise, see them as teachers rather than distractions. Release the urge to rush forward; instead, honour the quiet wisdom of your inner world. The clarity you gain today will support you in the weeks ahead.

Affirmation & Gratitude

"I honour my inner wisdom and trust that reflection leads me toward greater clarity and truth."

Gemini
30-January-2026

Energy lifts again today, Gemini, encouraging you to connect with friends or groups that share your vision. Collaboration will bring fresh inspiration, and your role as the communicator can help unify different perspectives. Be mindful of overextending yourself—sometimes, too many social or professional commitments scatter your focus. Choose gatherings that nourish your spirit and align with your long-term goals. Networking today could open a surprising opportunity, so be ready to follow up on meaningful conversations. The universe is opening doors through the people you meet.

Affirmation & Gratitude

"I am grateful for the connections that inspire me and the opportunities they bring into my life."

Gemini
31-January-2026

The cosmos turns your focus toward rest, solitude, and healing. After days of busy exchanges, today is best spent recharging. Pay attention to subtle insights through dreams, meditation, or quiet reflection. If you've been feeling drained, this is the universe reminding you to slow down and listen to your body and spirit. Sometimes the most productive thing you can do is step back and allow space for restoration. Trust that by nurturing yourself today, you'll return stronger and clearer for what's ahead.

Affirmation & Gratitude

"I give myself permission to rest, knowing renewal is part of my growth and strength."

February 2026

Gemini
01-February-2026

Gemini, a surge of energy arrives today, making it the perfect time to set intentions and embrace new beginnings. Your confidence is high, and your charm draws others to your ideas. Step forward with courage—you're being supported by the stars to take action on something important. This is also a day to trust your individuality; don't dilute your unique perspective to fit in. Your originality is your gift. What you start now has the potential to carry momentum for weeks to come.

Affirmation & Gratitude

"I am grateful for the fresh energy that inspires me to begin boldly and embrace my uniqueness."

Gemini
02-February-2026

Relationships come into focus, reminding you of the importance of balance and partnership. Whether in love, work, or friendship, the stars encourage cooperation today. Pay attention to both your needs and the needs of others—mutual respect will strengthen bonds. If disagreements arise, avoid defensiveness and instead focus on listening with empathy. Honest, heartfelt conversations will bring breakthroughs. This is also a good day to celebrate the people who walk alongside you on your path.

Affirmation & Gratitude

"I appreciate the balance of give and take that deepens and enriches my relationships."

Gemini

03-February-2026

Gemini, practical matters may call for attention today—finances, schedules, or health routines could feel especially pressing. While your airy nature prefers spontaneity, grounding yourself in practical action now will ease stress later. Approach tasks methodically, one step at a time, rather than scattering your energy across too many things at once. If you've been procrastinating, today offers the cosmic push to get organised. Think of this as fine-tuning the structure that supports your freedom.

Affirmation & Gratitude

"I am thankful for the discipline that keeps my life balanced and my energy flowing smoothly."

Gemini
04-February-2026

Adventure is calling again, Gemini, and the universe is urging you to expand your horizons. This may come through travel, study, or simply embracing a new philosophy or perspective. Your natural curiosity thrives when you explore beyond the familiar, and today is a reminder that growth comes from stretching your boundaries. Conversations with people from different walks of life may bring inspiration and broaden your understanding. Be open to new experiences—they could shift your trajectory in exciting ways.

Affirmation & Gratitude

"I embrace adventure and welcome new perspectives that enrich my journey."

Gemini
05-February-2026

Gemini, the stars highlight your career and public image today. You may feel the urge to step up, share your ideas, or demonstrate leadership. Recognition could come your way, whether through praise from a boss, acknowledgement from peers, or a sense of personal accomplishment. This is a good time to reflect on whether your daily actions align with your bigger ambitions. If they don't, make adjustments now—clarity will help you move forward with purpose. Don't underestimate your influence; others are watching and inspired by how you carry yourself.

Affirmation & Gratitude

"I am grateful for the recognition of my efforts and the confidence to pursue my bigger goals."

Gemini

06-February-2026

The cosmos turns your attention to rest and renewal, Gemini. After recent bursts of activity, today invites you to step back and recharge. Your mind may still be racing, but your body and spirit crave downtime. Trust that rest is not laziness—it's fuel for your next big move. Listen to your intuition and notice the subtle nudges guiding you; answers may surface in quiet moments. Creative inspiration is possible if you allow yourself space to breathe. Honour your need for balance and self-care.

Affirmation & Gratitude

"I value rest as an essential part of my journey, knowing it restores my clarity and energy."

Gemini

07-February-2026

Fresh energy arrives today, Gemini, giving you a boost of confidence and momentum. This is a day to focus on your individuality and express your authentic self without hesitation. Whether through creativity, work, or personal projects, you'll feel supported in taking bold steps forward. Others are drawn to your lively presence and quick thinking, so don't be surprised if you find yourself in the spotlight. Trust your instincts, but avoid spreading yourself too thin. One focused step will be more effective than juggling too many ideas.

Affirmation & Gratitude

"I celebrate my uniqueness and trust the universe to support me when I step into my true self."

Gemini
08-February-2026

Relationships and partnerships take centre stage. Gemini, you may be asked to compromise or negotiate today. While your instinct is to talk your way through situations, remember that listening deeply is just as important. Pay attention to the needs of those closest to you, whether in love, friendship, or business. This is a day for building bridges, strengthening trust, and aligning goals. If tension arises, see it as an opportunity to grow closer through honesty. Authentic connection will always be more rewarding than surface harmony.

Affirmation & Gratitude

"I am thankful for the trust and respect that build stronger, more loving relationships."

Gemini
09-February-2026

Practical matters rise to the top of your list today. Work tasks, financial details, or health-related responsibilities require your focus. While you prefer variety and change, Gemini, the stars ask you to ground yourself in routines that support long-term growth. Think of this as tending to the foundation of your life—the structures that allow you to thrive. If you've been delaying important decisions or avoiding details, now is the time to handle them. You'll feel lighter once these tasks are complete.

Affirmation & Gratitude

"I am grateful for the stability created through my consistent efforts and mindful choices."

Gemini
10-February-2026

Curiosity drives you strongly today, Gemini. You may feel pulled to explore something new—whether through travel, study, or engaging in deep conversations. Your mind craves stimulation, and this is a perfect day to feed it with fresh perspectives. Don't be afraid to step outside your comfort zone. Growth often comes when you allow yourself to learn from others and embrace experiences you've never tried before. Keep your heart and mind open—what you discover today could spark long-term inspiration.

Affirmation & Gratitude

"I embrace learning and new experiences, knowing they expand my world in beautiful ways."

Gemini
11-February-2026

Career matters and long-term goals are highlighted again today. You may feel a strong pull to make progress or set new intentions for where you're headed. Recognition is possible, but so is a wake-up call if you've been veering off track. The universe is asking you to refine your vision and ensure your actions align with your ambitions. Don't be afraid to take responsibility for your direction—you're more capable than you realise. Step forward with both confidence and humility.

Affirmation & Gratitude

"I am thankful for clarity in my goals and the strength to keep moving toward my dreams."

Gemini
12-February-2026

Gemini, the stars invite you into introspection today. Your usually busy mind may crave silence, and that's no accident—the universe wants you to slow down and reconnect with your inner world. Dreams, signs, or flashes of intuition may feel stronger now, so pay attention. This is an ideal day to meditate, journal, or simply unplug from the constant flow of information. If you feel restless, remember that slowing down allows deeper clarity to emerge. What feels unclear now will reveal itself when you allow stillness to guide you.

Affirmation & Gratitude

"I am grateful for quiet moments that restore my balance and connect me with my inner wisdom."

Gemini
13-February-2026

A burst of lively energy returns, Gemini, reminding you how magnetic and inspiring you can be when you step into your authentic self. Today encourages self-expression—through words, creativity, or even the way you carry yourself. Others are drawn to your spark, and opportunities may appear simply because of your openness and charm. Don't hold back from sharing what makes you unique. However, avoid scattering your energy; focus on one outlet where your brilliance can truly shine. The world needs your voice today—let it be heard.

Affirmation & Gratitude

"I celebrate my individuality and express my true self with joy and confidence."

Gemini

14-February-2026

Valentine's Day carries extra emphasis for you this year, Gemini. The stars spotlight relationships, and whether single or partnered, the focus is on love in all its forms. Expect heartfelt conversations, opportunities for deeper connection, or perhaps surprising insights into what you truly value in others. If tensions arise, they can be softened with honesty and laughter—your natural gifts. Today is less about grand gestures and more about authentic exchanges. Celebrate love not only with others, but also with yourself.

Affirmation & Gratitude

"I am grateful for the love that flows into my life, in big and small ways."

Gemini
15-February-2026

Practical energy takes the stage today. Gemini, you may feel the need to bring order to your routines, finances, or workspace. While your adaptable nature thrives on change, creating structure now will actually help you feel freer in the long run. Tackle lingering tasks you've been putting off; you'll feel lighter once they're done. Health and wellness are also highlighted, making this a good day to check in with your body and commit to small, sustainable habits.

Affirmation & Gratitude

"I am thankful for the order and consistency that support my energy and wellbeing."

Gemini

16-February-2026

Adventure is calling again, Gemini, and the stars push you toward learning, exploring, and expanding your horizons. This may come through travel, diving into a new subject, or engaging with people whose perspectives differ from yours. Your mind thrives on variety, and today offers the chance to feed it with rich, inspiring experiences. Don't be afraid to challenge your old beliefs or routines—growth happens when you step outside your familiar box.

Affirmation & Gratitude

"I embrace exploration and new ideas, knowing they expand my understanding of the world and myself."

Gemini
17-February-2026

Career matters and long-term ambitions are spotlighted today. You may feel pushed to take charge of a situation, prove your skills, or clarify your path. Recognition is possible, but equally, you may see where more effort or adjustments are needed. Don't let self-doubt creep in—this is your chance to step forward with confidence. Your natural adaptability makes you well-suited to handle challenges. If guidance from a mentor or superior appears, take it seriously—it could shape your next steps.

Affirmation & Gratitude

"I am grateful for the clarity and direction that guide me toward meaningful achievements."

Gemini
18-February-2026

The cosmos invites you inward again, Gemini, encouraging reflection and spiritual awareness. After recent bursts of external activity, this is a day for checking in with your inner compass. Dreams or subtle insights may carry important messages. Pay attention to what your body and emotions are telling you—they're pointing toward what needs care and balance. Avoid rushing or forcing results; trust the process unfolding behind the scenes. Sometimes progress comes not from doing, but from being present.

Affirmation & Gratitude

"I honour the wisdom within me and trust the quiet voice that guides my journey."

Gemini
19-February-2026

Gemini, today the Sun shifts into Pisces, drawing your attention toward career, reputation, and long-term ambitions. You may feel a renewed desire to align your work with your deeper sense of purpose. Pay attention to opportunities that arise now, as they could lead to lasting recognition. This is also a day to review how your personal values show up in your professional life. Are you pursuing goals that truly resonate with your heart, or simply following expectations? Let authenticity guide your next steps, and you'll feel both fulfilled and motivated.

Affirmation & Gratitude

"I align my ambitions with my true values, allowing purpose to guide my professional path."

Gemini

20-February-2026

Your friendships and group connections are highlighted today, Gemini. Collaboration feels natural, and your ability to communicate clearly makes you the bridge between different perspectives. Expect lively exchanges and perhaps even the spark of a new project. Be mindful, however, of overextending yourself; not every group or cause requires your full energy. Choose to invest your time where it feels most rewarding and aligned with your long-term goals. A conversation today could connect you to someone who plays a key role in your journey ahead.

Affirmation & Gratitude

"I am grateful for communities that inspire and support me in reaching higher together."

Gemini
21-February-2026

Gemini, the universe calls you to rest and restore today. After days of social and professional activity, your spirit craves stillness. Don't ignore that tug to retreat—it's the cosmos reminding you that balance is essential. This is a day to recharge, perhaps through meditation, journaling, or simply quiet reflection. Subtle insights may come through dreams or inner nudges, helping you see situations in a new light. Honour the need for solitude without guilt; tomorrow's energy will call you outward again, and you'll feel refreshed for it.

Affirmation & Gratitude

"I allow myself the gift of rest, knowing it replenishes my spirit and clears my mind."

Gemini
22-February-2026

The energy shifts back into vibrancy today, Gemini, giving you a boost of confidence and charisma. You may feel ready to tackle personal goals, express your creativity, or take a step that highlights your individuality. People are drawn to your spark and may look to you for leadership or inspiration. Trust your instincts, and don't be afraid to stand out. You don't need to conform—your uniqueness is exactly what makes you valuable. Use this surge of energy to move something forward with courage and enthusiasm.

Affirmation & Gratitude

"I celebrate my individuality and step boldly into the spotlight of my life."

Gemini
23-February-2026

Relationships are in focus, and the stars encourage honest exchanges, Gemini. You may find that someone close to you seeks reassurance or clarity. Rather than skimming the surface with light banter, today is about diving deeper into truth. Whether it's love, friendship, or partnership, strengthening trust is key. Avoid deflecting uncomfortable conversations—face them with patience and openness. By doing so, you'll create a foundation of respect and understanding that lasts well beyond today. Harmony is built on authenticity, not avoidance.

Affirmation & Gratitude

"I appreciate honesty in my relationships and value the trust it creates."

Gemini
24-February-2026

Today's energy brings attention to routines, health, and responsibilities. Gemini, while you thrive on variety, the stars are nudging you to focus on consistency. Review your daily habits —are they supporting or draining you? Small improvements, whether in diet, exercise, or organisation, will have long-lasting benefits. Don't let the details overwhelm you; instead, approach them one step at a time. By tending to these practical matters, you'll free yourself for greater flexibility and joy in other areas of life.

Affirmation & Gratitude

"I am grateful for the habits and routines that keep me grounded and energised."

Gemini
25-February-2026

Adventure is in the air, Gemini, and the universe is encouraging you to seek new horizons. This could come through travel, study, or connecting with someone who expands your worldview. Your curiosity is your compass, and today it points you toward experiences that spark inspiration and growth. Don't dismiss an opportunity just because it feels unfamiliar. By stepping outside your comfort zone, you'll uncover insights and possibilities you never imagined. Growth happens when you allow yourself to stretch beyond the ordinary.

Affirmation & Gratitude

"I welcome new experiences with curiosity, trusting they expand my understanding of life and myself."

Gemini
26-February-2026

Gemini, career and public recognition take the spotlight today. You may feel a strong push to demonstrate your abilities, step into leadership, or showcase your ideas. Recognition from authority figures or peers is likely, and your natural charm helps you shine in professional spaces. However, don't let the desire for approval distract you from your authentic path. The stars remind you that true success comes when your ambitions align with your inner values. Take pride in your progress while also clarifying your next big steps.

Affirmation & Gratitude

"I am grateful for opportunities that allow me to shine while staying true to my authentic path."

Gemini
27-February-2026

The cosmos encourages you to slow down and look inward today. After recent focus on external achievements, your spirit may crave reflection. This is a day to rest, release pressure, and listen closely to your inner guidance. Subtle messages may surface through dreams, meditation, or even quiet moments in nature. Don't rush or force clarity—sometimes answers arrive when you create space for them. You may also feel called to let go of something that no longer serves you, clearing the way for what's next.

Affirmation & Gratitude

"I honour rest and reflection, trusting that clarity will emerge in its own perfect time."

Gemini

28-February-2026

A surge of energy returns, Gemini, boosting your confidence and reminding you of your unique gifts. This is a day for self-expression, creativity, and fresh starts. Others are drawn to your light-hearted nature and quick wit, so don't hesitate to step into the spotlight. Whether in personal projects or professional settings, your voice has power. Focus your energy on what excites you most rather than scattering it too widely. The universe is supporting bold moves—trust your instincts and lead with enthusiasm.

Affirmation & Gratitude

"I celebrate my uniqueness and share my gifts with confidence and joy."

March 2026

Gemini

01-March-2026

Relationships take centre stage today, Gemini. You may feel the need to balance your independence with partnership or collaboration. Open communication is your greatest ally—share your perspective honestly, but also listen deeply to others. This is a good day to smooth over past misunderstandings or strengthen bonds through thoughtful gestures. If single, you may encounter someone who sparks your curiosity in unexpected ways. Remember, relationships grow best when nurtured with both honesty and patience.

Affirmation & Gratitude

"I am thankful for the relationships that bring balance, love, and learning into my life."

Gemini
02-March-2026

The energy today shifts toward health, work routines, and daily responsibilities. Gemini, your flexible spirit sometimes resists structure, but the stars highlight the importance of consistency. Focus on small, steady improvements—whether organising your workspace, fine-tuning finances, or caring for your body. Avoid overcomplicating things; simplicity is your ally today. By paying attention to details now, you'll create a stronger foundation for bigger goals later. Balance is key—honour your responsibilities while also making space for joy.

Affirmation & Gratitude

"I am grateful for routines and habits that support my wellbeing and success."

Gemini
03-March-2026

Adventure calls again, Gemini, and your curiosity is buzzing. Today is ideal for expanding your horizons through learning, travel, or meaningful conversations with people from different walks of life. You thrive on variety, and stepping into something new will inspire fresh insights. Don't be afraid to challenge your old perspectives or try something unfamiliar—growth lies outside your comfort zone. The universe is reminding you that your mind is your greatest tool, and feeding it with new experiences fuels your spirit.

Affirmation & Gratitude

"I welcome new adventures and the wisdom they bring into my life."

Gemini

04-March-2026

Career matters and long-term ambitions resurface today. Gemini, you may receive recognition for your efforts or feel inspired to set new goals. This is a day for strategy—consider the direction you're heading and how your daily choices align with your bigger vision. Authority figures or mentors may play a role, offering guidance or opening doors for you. Step forward with confidence, but stay grounded in your authentic values. Success is not only about achievement—it's about alignment with who you truly are.

Affirmation & Gratitude

"I am thankful for clarity in my goals and the opportunities that support my growth."

Gemini
05-March-2026

Gemini, today invites you into a quieter space of reflection. While you often thrive in conversation and activity, the stars nudge you to slow down and tune into your inner world. Dreams, subtle signs, or intuitive feelings may carry important messages. This isn't the time to rush decisions—let insights unfold naturally. Consider journaling or meditating to process emotions that may have been pushed aside. By honouring your inner voice, you'll find clarity about your next steps. Your intuition is strong now—trust it.

Affirmation & Gratitude

"I listen to my inner wisdom, trusting it to guide me toward clarity and truth."

Gemini
06-March-2026

Fresh energy flows into your life, Gemini, reigniting your confidence and motivation. This is a day to step into your individuality and share your gifts with the world. You may feel drawn to begin a new project, take on a leadership role, or simply express yourself more boldly. Others are noticing your spark and may be inspired by your words or actions. Don't hold back—your authenticity is magnetic. Focus your energy rather than scattering it, and you'll see meaningful progress.

Affirmation & Gratitude
"I celebrate my individuality and allow my authentic self to shine brightly."

Gemini
07-March-2026

Partnerships take focus today, and you may feel the need to strengthen bonds through honest communication and compromise. Gemini, you're gifted at finding the right words, but today requires active listening too. Pay attention to what others are really saying beneath the surface. Whether in love, friendship, or business, today is about building trust and working together. If tensions appear, don't shy away—they are opportunities to deepen understanding. Connection flourishes when truth and patience meet.

Affirmation & Gratitude

"I appreciate the balance and growth that come from meaningful partnerships."

Gemini
08-March-2026

Gemini, the stars shine on your routines, health, and responsibilities today. You may feel called to refine your daily structure, organise tasks, or check in with your wellbeing. While variety excites you, the cosmos reminds you that consistent habits give you freedom in the long run. A small step taken today—like preparing healthy meals, scheduling exercise, or clearing clutter—will ripple into lasting benefits. Productivity feels easier when you stay grounded and focused on one task at a time.

Affirmation & Gratitude

"I am thankful for routines that nurture my energy and keep me balanced."

Gemini
09-March-2026

Curiosity surges, urging you to seek out new knowledge, experiences, or adventures. The universe encourages you to stretch beyond the familiar, Gemini, whether through study, travel, or conversations that broaden your perspective. Your mind is sharp and eager, making this an excellent time for learning or exploring ideas that inspire growth. Don't ignore opportunities that feel a little intimidating—they're often the ones that expand you most. By following your curiosity, you unlock doors to exciting possibilities.

Affirmation & Gratitude

"I embrace new experiences with curiosity, knowing they expand my mind and spirit."

Gemini

10-March-2026

Your career and long-term goals come into sharp focus today. Recognition for your efforts may arrive, or you may feel motivated to refine your ambitions. Gemini, your natural adaptability makes you skilled at juggling opportunities, but today you're encouraged to think strategically. Where do you see yourself in five years? Align your current choices with that vision. Conversations with mentors or colleagues could provide valuable insight—don't dismiss their guidance. Step confidently toward your future; the stars are supporting you.

Affirmation & Gratitude

"I am grateful for clarity in my ambitions and the opportunities guiding me toward success."

Gemini
11-March-2026

The cosmos calls you inward again, asking you to reflect on the balance between your outer achievements and inner wellbeing. You may feel a little quieter today, preferring solitude or creative outlets over socialising. This is a time to nurture your spiritual and emotional health. Pay attention to subtle signs—they could reveal the next step on your path. Avoid forcing results; let things unfold naturally. When you allow yourself space to recharge, inspiration flows more freely.

Affirmation & Gratitude

"I honour my need for rest and reflection, knowing it restores balance and clarity."

Gemini
12-March-2026

Gemini, today brings a fresh wave of energy into your life, reminding you of the power of authenticity and self-expression. You may feel an urge to speak up, showcase your talents, or take a bold step forward with a project. The world is paying attention to you, so don't shrink yourself to fit in. Your natural wit, charm, and adaptability make you magnetic, and people will gravitate toward your ideas. Use this momentum to set intentions that truly align with your passions.

Affirmation & Gratitude

"I embrace my individuality and trust that my authentic voice inspires others."

Gemini
13-March-2026

Relationships are highlighted, Gemini, and you may be called to find balance between your needs and those of others. Today's energy favours cooperation and compromise, but it also reminds you not to lose yourself in the process. Whether in love, friendship, or business, focus on honest communication and mutual respect. If misunderstandings arise, your ability to lighten the mood and find common ground will smooth tensions. Partnerships can grow stronger when nurtured with patience, humour, and truth.

Affirmation & Gratitude

"I am thankful for partnerships that teach me balance, growth, and mutual respect."

Gemini
14-March-2026

The cosmos asks you to turn attention toward your routines, responsibilities, and health. While you often prefer spontaneity, today is about creating stability in the little things. Organising your schedule, tackling a task you've put off, or committing to self-care practices will serve you well. Pay attention to how your body responds to stress—you may need to slow down or make small adjustments that improve your overall wellbeing. Grounding yourself in practical action today brings long-term freedom.

Affirmation & Gratitude

"I value the routines that support my wellbeing and keep my energy flowing smoothly."

Gemini
15-March-2026

Adventure is calling, Gemini, and your restless spirit craves variety. This is an excellent day to explore, whether through travel, study, or diving into new ideas. Conversations with people from different backgrounds may inspire you, offering perspectives that expand your worldview. Don't be afraid to challenge old beliefs—you grow when you step beyond the familiar. Feed your curiosity, and you'll discover opportunities for personal growth and inspiration that carry you far beyond today.

Affirmation & Gratitude

"I welcome new experiences, trusting they expand my horizons and enrich my life."

Gemini
16-March-2026

Gemini, your career and ambitions come into focus again. You may feel driven to prove yourself, showcase your skills, or refine your goals. Recognition is possible, but the deeper question is: does your current path align with your true values? This is a day for clarity, not just achievement. Seek guidance if needed—mentors or colleagues may offer advice that helps you see the bigger picture. Take time to plan strategically, aligning your daily actions with your long-term vision.

Affirmation & Gratitude

"I am grateful for the clarity and opportunities that guide me toward meaningful success."

Gemini
17-March-2026

Today, the cosmos encourages you to turn inward and rest. Gemini, you thrive on activity, but constant motion drains you. This is a day to restore balance through quiet reflection, creative pursuits, or simply doing less. Your intuition is sharp now—pay attention to subtle messages that may surface in dreams or passing thoughts. By slowing down, you'll gain insights that help you prepare for what's next. Honour your need for peace and allow yourself to recharge fully.

Affirmation & Gratitude

"I honour rest as a vital part of my journey, trusting it restores clarity and energy."

Gemini
18-March-2026

Fresh energy surges again, Gemini, filling you with confidence and motivation. This is the perfect time to launch something new or revisit a project with renewed enthusiasm. Your charm and adaptability attract people to your ideas, so don't be surprised if support or collaboration appears. The stars encourage you to focus your energy rather than scattering it. When you choose one path and commit, you'll make tangible progress. Today is about being bold, expressive, and unapologetically yourself.

Affirmation & Gratitude

"I celebrate my unique energy and step forward with courage and authenticity."

Gemini
19-March-2026

Gemini, today places a spotlight on your relationships. The stars are encouraging you to look honestly at how balanced your partnerships feel. Are you giving too much without receiving enough in return, or perhaps holding back when more openness is needed? This is a good day for heartfelt conversations that strengthen bonds. Use your natural gift for communication to express yourself clearly, but also take the time to listen deeply. Stronger trust and mutual understanding can emerge when honesty is paired with patience and kindness.

Affirmation & Gratitude

"I am grateful for relationships that grow stronger through honesty, respect, and understanding."

Gemini
20-March-2026

The cosmos directs your attention toward your daily responsibilities and wellbeing. Gemini, while your airy energy prefers variety and freedom, today reminds you of the value of consistency. Small, practical actions—like organising your space, planning your week, or focusing on your health—can create big shifts in how supported you feel. Don't try to tackle everything at once; instead, choose one or two priorities and give them your full attention. By grounding your energy, you'll create more stability to support your curiosity and flexibility.

Affirmation & Gratitude

"I am thankful for the routines that bring balance, structure, and ease into my life."

Gemini
21-March-2026

Gemini, adventure is calling, and your spirit feels restless for change. Whether it's travel, studying something new, or even exploring a new perspective, today is about expansion. Conversations with people outside your usual circle may spark surprising insights. You thrive on curiosity, and the stars encourage you to follow it boldly. Don't hesitate to try something unfamiliar—it could be the very thing that shifts your trajectory. Growth doesn't always come from planning; sometimes it's about saying yes to the unknown.

Affirmation & Gratitude
"I welcome new opportunities to expand my horizons and embrace the lessons they bring."

Gemini
22-March-2026

Career matters come into focus today, Gemini. You may feel recognition for your efforts or a push to clarify your ambitions. While it's tempting to juggle multiple paths, the stars encourage you to focus on what aligns most with your heart and long-term vision. You don't have to have it all figured out, but clarity about your priorities will help you take purposeful steps. Authority figures or mentors may play a role now, offering valuable guidance or opening doors.

Affirmation & Gratitude

"I am grateful for clarity in my career path and the guidance that helps me grow."

Gemini

23-March-2026

Gemini, today calls for reflection and rest. After recent busyness, your body and spirit may crave quiet. This is a day to pause, reflect, and allow your intuition to guide you. You may find answers surfacing in dreams, meditation, or quiet moments. Don't dismiss the subtle messages—the universe often whispers guidance when you finally slow down enough to hear it. Avoid overloading yourself with tasks; honouring your need for stillness today will restore balance and energy for the days ahead.

Affirmation & Gratitude

"I honour the gift of stillness, knowing it connects me to wisdom and peace."

Gemini
24-March-2026

Fresh energy fills the air today, Gemini, encouraging you to step into your individuality and shine. This is a day for self-expression and courage—whether through creative projects, bold ideas, or simply showing up authentically in your interactions. Your natural wit and charm make you magnetic, and people are likely to notice. Focus on one key area where you can make progress instead of scattering your energy. The stars remind you that your uniqueness is your power—don't hold back from sharing it.

Affirmation & Gratitude

"I celebrate my uniqueness and embrace the courage to share it fully."

Gemini
25-March-2026

Partnerships are emphasised again today, and the stars ask you to pay attention to balance and reciprocity. Gemini, your ability to see multiple perspectives makes you a natural mediator, but don't overlook your own needs in the process. If something feels out of alignment, now is the time to address it gently but clearly. This is also a good day for collaboration—working with someone else could lead to a breakthrough. Trust that honest exchanges will strengthen bonds, even if they feel uncomfortable at first.

Affirmation & Gratitude

"I am grateful for partnerships that grow stronger through trust, openness, and mutual respect."

Gemini
26-March-2026

Gemini, today's energy turns your focus toward the details of life—your routines, responsibilities, and health. While your adaptable spirit prefers variety, the cosmos encourages structure now. Don't underestimate the power of small, consistent actions. Tidying your space, planning meals, or refining your daily schedule may feel minor, but they create stability that supports your freedom. Avoid scattering your energy by trying to do everything at once. Pick one practical task and complete it fully—you'll feel accomplished and lighter for it. These small steps will ripple into long-term balance and wellbeing.

Affirmation & Gratitude

"I am grateful for the stability created through small, consistent actions each day."

Gemini
27-March-2026

Adventure beckons, Gemini, and the stars urge you to stretch beyond the familiar. This is a day for new experiences, whether through travel, exploring fresh ideas, or connecting with people from different cultures. Your mind thrives when fed with variety, and today offers the chance to expand your perspective. Say yes to something that excites your curiosity, even if it feels a little intimidating. Growth happens when you leave your comfort zone. Inspiration from today could spark a long-term interest or opportunity that reshapes your path.

Affirmation & Gratitude

"I welcome new experiences with curiosity, knowing they expand my mind and spirit."

Gemini
28-March-2026

Gemini, career and ambitions step into the spotlight again. Recognition for your work may come, or you may feel the push to set clearer goals. The universe is asking you to evaluate whether your current direction truly aligns with your long-term vision. If not, now is the time to make adjustments. A mentor, boss, or colleague may offer feedback—listen closely, as it could open important doors. Your ability to adapt makes you well-suited to seize opportunities when they appear. Stand tall and trust your instincts.

Affirmation & Gratitude

"I am thankful for the clarity and recognition guiding my path toward meaningful success."

Gemini
29-March-2026

The cosmos calls you inward, Gemini. Today favours rest, reflection, and tuning into your inner world. While you often thrive on interaction and movement, stillness can be just as powerful. Pay attention to intuitive nudges and signs—they may reveal what your conscious mind has been overlooking. This is a good day to journal, meditate, or simply give yourself permission to unplug. Avoid rushing into decisions. By slowing down, you create space for deeper wisdom to surface, preparing you for the days ahead.

Affirmation & Gratitude

"I honour my need for rest, trusting stillness to guide me toward clarity."

Gemini
30-March-2026

Energy lifts again today, filling you with confidence and self-expression. Gemini, this is a day to step into your individuality and embrace what makes you unique. Your charisma is magnetic, and people are naturally drawn to your light-hearted approach. Don't dilute yourself to fit into expectations—your originality is your strength. Whether starting a new project, sharing your ideas, or simply showing up fully as yourself, you'll find momentum building. The stars remind you to act boldly, trusting your instincts to lead you forward.

Affirmation & Gratitude

"I celebrate my individuality and trust my authentic voice to guide my path."

Gemini
31-March-2026

Relationships and partnerships come into focus, Gemini. Today asks you to balance your independence with cooperation. You may find yourself navigating compromise or having heartfelt conversations that deepen trust. If tensions arise, avoid deflecting with humour and instead listen with empathy. This is an excellent day for collaboration or strengthening a bond by being honest about your needs. Remember, partnerships thrive when both sides feel seen and heard. By giving space for openness, you'll create harmony that lasts.

Affirmation & Gratitude

"I am grateful for the harmony and growth that come from honest, balanced partnerships."

April 2026

Gemini
01-April-2026

Practical responsibilities call your attention today. Gemini, your curious mind loves freedom, but the stars highlight the importance of discipline now. Focus on tasks you may have been avoiding—sorting finances, planning routines, or addressing health matters. While these may not feel exciting, they are the foundations that support your bigger dreams. Think of today as maintenance work for your life. By tending to these details, you create freedom and flexibility in the future. Steady effort will bring long-lasting rewards.

Affirmation & Gratitude

"I appreciate the discipline and structure that allow me to thrive in all areas of life."

Gemini
02-April-2026

Gemini, your adventurous spirit is stirring again, and the stars encourage you to expand your horizons. This could come through study, travel, or simply diving into conversations that stretch your perspective. Your natural curiosity thrives when you engage with new ideas, and today offers inspiration in abundance. Don't hesitate to step outside your comfort zone, even if it feels a little uncertain. What you learn now may spark an exciting long-term path. Keep your mind open—the universe is offering insights that broaden your world in meaningful ways.

Affirmation & Gratitude

"I welcome adventure and learning, knowing every new experience enriches my life."

Gemini
03-April-2026

Career and ambition take centre stage today, Gemini. You may receive recognition for your efforts, or feel the push to clarify your long-term direction. This is a powerful time to assess whether your daily actions align with the bigger vision you hold for yourself. Mentors or authority figures could offer advice—listen carefully, as their guidance might shape your next steps. The stars support strategic planning now, so think about where you want to be and map a path to get there.

Affirmation & Gratitude

"I am thankful for clarity in my career goals and for opportunities that support my growth."

Gemini
04-April-2026

Gemini, today invites you to rest and reflect. After days of outward focus, the cosmos calls you inward to recharge your spirit. Trust that slowing down is productive—it gives space for insights to surface. Pay attention to dreams, signs, or intuitive feelings; they may reveal hidden truths. Avoid filling your schedule with too much noise. Instead, allow stillness to guide you. By honouring your inner needs, you restore balance and clarity, preparing yourself for the fresh energy soon to come.

Affirmation & Gratitude

"I honour rest as essential, trusting stillness to guide me toward clarity and peace."

Gemini
05-April-2026

A surge of energy fills the air today, Gemini, giving you confidence and vitality. This is a day to take action, express your individuality, and embrace your unique talents. Whether starting something new or pushing forward with a project, your momentum is strong. People notice your charisma and may be drawn to your ideas, so don't hold back. Focus your energy rather than scattering it—you'll see more progress when you commit to one direction fully. The universe supports bold, authentic moves today.

Affirmation & Gratitude

"I celebrate my individuality and the courage to act on my authentic desires."

Gemini
06-April-2026

Relationships are highlighted, Gemini, and the stars encourage balance and cooperation. Today favours honest exchanges and meaningful conversations that strengthen trust. If you've been avoiding a difficult topic, this is the time to gently bring it forward. Use your gift for communication, but also make space to listen. Whether in love, friendship, or partnership, harmony grows when both sides feel seen and valued. Your ability to connect deeply is a powerful tool—use it to create understanding and unity.

Affirmation & Gratitude

"I value the honesty and respect that create strong and meaningful connections."

Gemini
07-April-2026

Gemini, practical energy fills the day, directing your attention to responsibilities and routines. While you prefer variety, the cosmos reminds you of the power of consistency. This is a good day to focus on health, organisation, or financial planning. Take a step you've been putting off—small, steady improvements will make a big difference over time. Productivity flows easily when you focus on one task at a time instead of juggling too many at once. The structure you create today supports your freedom tomorrow.

Affirmation & Gratitude

"I am grateful for routines that support my wellbeing and future growth."

Gemini
08-April-2026

Adventure stirs again, and you may feel restless for something new. Gemini, this is a day to explore beyond your familiar routine, whether through travel, study, or diving into new philosophies. Conversations with people who see the world differently may inspire you and shift your perspective. Don't shy away from the unknown—it holds the keys to growth. When you follow your curiosity, you open yourself to opportunities that expand not only your mind but also your spirit. Trust where your instincts lead.

Affirmation & Gratitude

"I welcome new perspectives and embrace experiences that broaden my understanding."

Gemini
09-April-2026

Gemini, today brings your career and ambitions into focus again. You may feel ready to take a bold step forward or receive recognition for your contributions. The cosmos asks you to think strategically—what are your long-term goals, and are your daily choices supporting them? This is a day for aligning action with vision. Authority figures or mentors may offer advice, and listening with an open mind could spark clarity. Don't be afraid to claim your place in the spotlight; your adaptability and charm make you well-suited to lead with authenticity.

Affirmation & Gratitude

"I am grateful for clarity in my ambitions and the courage to pursue my goals."

Gemini
10-April-2026

The energy shifts inward today, Gemini, inviting you to slow down and reflect. After recent focus on external achievements, your soul craves peace and solitude. This is a day to connect with your intuition and explore your inner world. Journaling, meditation, or simply allowing space for silence will be powerful. Pay attention to subtle messages or gut feelings—they carry wisdom that logic alone cannot provide. By honouring your need for rest, you'll return with renewed clarity and strength. Trust that slowing down is part of moving forward.

Affirmation & Gratitude

"I honour stillness and trust my inner wisdom to guide my path."

Gemini
11-April-2026

Fresh energy arrives, Gemini, lifting your spirit and filling you with confidence. You may feel drawn to begin something new or revisit a project with enthusiasm. This is a day for bold self-expression—your words and ideas carry power, and people are likely to notice. Step forward with authenticity and courage; you don't need to conform to anyone else's expectations. The stars are supporting progress, but remember to focus your energy rather than scattering it in too many directions. One decisive action today can create lasting impact.

Affirmation & Gratitude

"I celebrate my individuality and take bold steps toward my dreams."

Gemini
12-April-2026

Relationships take centre stage today, Gemini. The cosmos highlights the importance of balance, compromise, and communication. You may be asked to see things from another's perspective or address an issue that's been simmering beneath the surface. Use your natural gift for words, but pair it with deep listening. Partnerships can grow stronger through openness, honesty, and a willingness to meet in the middle. If single, you may notice opportunities for new connections through shared interests or meaningful conversations.

Affirmation & Gratitude

"I am grateful for partnerships built on trust, respect, and genuine connection."

Gemini
13-April-2026

Gemini, practical matters call for attention today—finances, health, and responsibilities may demand your focus. While you often prefer spontaneity, today is about grounding your energy. Small, consistent steps will lead to long-term stability. Don't try to juggle everything; instead, prioritise the most important tasks and handle them steadily. Taking care of these practical details frees your mind and spirit for the variety and adventure you love. Think of today as strengthening your foundation so you can build with confidence tomorrow.

Affirmation & Gratitude

"I am thankful for the balance that practical action brings to my life."

Gemini
14-April-2026

Adventure is calling again, Gemini, and the stars are urging you to expand your perspective. This could be through travel, education, or engaging in conversations that challenge your usual way of thinking. Your mind thrives on stimulation, and today offers it in abundance. Don't shy away from stepping outside your comfort zone—growth often comes from unfamiliar paths. Follow your curiosity, and you may discover inspiration that sparks exciting new directions. The world feels wide open today—embrace it fully.

Affirmation & Gratitude

"I welcome new experiences that expand my horizons and inspire my growth."

Gemini
15-April-2026

Career and recognition are in focus today. Gemini, you may feel a push to showcase your talents or refine your goals. Authority figures may notice your efforts, offering support or feedback that guides your path. This is a day for aligning your ambitions with authenticity. Success will come not just from achievement, but from pursuing what feels true to you. Step confidently into opportunities that arise, but remember: integrity is what ensures your impact lasts.

Affirmation & Gratitude

"I am grateful for opportunities that align with my true purpose and values."

Gemini
16-April-2026

Gemini, today the cosmos draws you inward, asking you to pause and reconnect with your inner self. After recent focus on external achievements and responsibilities, your spirit craves reflection. You may feel more sensitive to subtle energies, dreams, or intuitive nudges —pay attention, for they hold wisdom. This is not the day to push hard or overextend yourself. Instead, honour rest and self-care. Creative pursuits, meditation, or journaling can reveal insights that guide your next steps. By slowing down, you allow clarity to rise naturally.

Affirmation & Gratitude

"I honour rest and reflection, trusting my inner wisdom to guide me."

Gemini
17-April-2026

Fresh energy fills your day, Gemini, making you feel confident and ready to shine. This is a perfect time to express your individuality, take bold action, and share your ideas. Your charm and wit are magnetic, drawing others to you. Opportunities for leadership or recognition may appear, so step forward with courage. Focus your energy on one clear path rather than scattering it across too many projects. When you commit fully, you create powerful momentum. The stars encourage you to embrace your uniqueness and trust your instincts.

Affirmation & Gratitude

"I celebrate my individuality and courageously share my light with the world."

Gemini
18-April-2026

Relationships are highlighted, Gemini, and the stars encourage balance and connection. Today favours collaboration, heartfelt conversations, and deepening bonds. Whether with a partner, friend, or colleague, you may need to compromise or listen more closely. Your ability to communicate with humour and clarity is a gift—use it wisely. Don't avoid difficult conversations; facing them honestly can strengthen trust. This is also a good day to celebrate the relationships that bring joy and stability into your life. Remember, harmony comes from honesty, not avoidance.

Affirmation & Gratitude

"I am thankful for the love and respect that strengthen my connections."

Gemini
19-April-2026

Practical energy fills the day, urging you to focus on routines, organisation, and wellbeing. Gemini, while you thrive on spontaneity, structure helps you flourish in the long run. Take small, steady steps toward tidying your environment, refining your schedule, or caring for your health. This is a productive time to handle details you may have overlooked. Don't try to do everything at once—choose one priority and give it your full attention. The foundation you build today will support your freedom and flexibility tomorrow.

Affirmation & Gratitude
"I am grateful for the balance and order that daily habits bring into my life."

Gemini
20-April-2026

Gemini, today your adventurous side is stirred, and you're encouraged to step beyond the familiar. This could mean travel, studying something new, or exploring a fresh perspective through conversation. Your mind thrives when challenged, and today offers inspiration to expand your worldview. Don't hesitate to say yes to opportunities that feel exciting yet slightly daunting—they hold the key to growth. The universe reminds you that curiosity is your greatest compass. Follow it boldly, and you'll uncover new possibilities.

Affirmation & Gratitude

"I welcome new adventures and the wisdom they bring into my life."

Gemini
21-April-2026

Career and long-term goals come into focus today. Recognition for your work is possible, or you may feel motivated to refine your ambitions. Gemini, while your adaptability allows you to juggle many roles, the stars encourage you to focus on what truly matters. Align your daily actions with your long-term vision, and you'll see momentum build. Guidance from a mentor or colleague may prove valuable—don't ignore their input. Stand tall in your confidence and let your authenticity shine through every step you take.

Affirmation & Gratitude

"I am grateful for clarity in my ambitions and the courage to pursue them."

Gemini

22-April-2026

The cosmos encourages reflection today, Gemini. You may feel quieter, craving solitude or simply space to process emotions. Intuition is heightened, and subtle insights may come through dreams, inner nudges, or quiet contemplation. Avoid pushing yourself into constant activity—this is a day for rest and inner connection. By slowing down, you create room for wisdom to surface naturally. Trust that even in stillness, progress is being made. Your inner world is just as important as your outer achievements. Honour both equally.

Affirmation & Gratitude

"I trust my inner wisdom and honour the peace that reflection brings."

Gemini
23-April-2026

Gemini, today brings a fresh burst of confidence and vitality. You may feel ready to step into the spotlight, share your talents, or take on a leadership role. The stars remind you that your individuality is your strength—don't water yourself down to fit in. Your ideas have power, and others are more receptive than you may realise. Use this surge of energy to make meaningful progress on a project or to start something bold. Your authenticity inspires those around you—own it proudly.

Affirmation & Gratitude

"I celebrate my individuality and trust my authenticity to guide my success."

Gemini

24-April-2026

Relationships and partnerships are highlighted, Gemini. Today encourages balance, cooperation, and heartfelt exchanges. If you've been skimming the surface, this is a day for deeper connection. A conversation may clear lingering misunderstandings, or you may find clarity about the direction of a relationship. Remember, true harmony isn't about avoiding conflict—it's about addressing issues with patience and honesty. Your natural humour can lighten tense moments, but don't avoid what needs to be said. Stronger bonds are built on authenticity.

Affirmation & Gratitude

"I am grateful for the honesty and trust that strengthen my relationships."

Gemini

25-April-2026

Practical matters demand your attention today. Gemini, you may need to tackle responsibilities related to finances, work, or health. While these tasks may feel mundane compared to your love of variety, they are the foundation that supports your freedom. Focus on consistency and small, manageable steps rather than trying to handle everything at once. Productivity flows when you give yourself structure. By attending to the details today, you'll feel lighter and more prepared for future adventures.

Affirmation & Gratitude

"I am thankful for the structure that supports my wellbeing and long-term growth."

Gemini
26-April-2026

Gemini, your adventurous side stirs once again, and the universe is encouraging exploration. Whether through travel, study, or exposure to new ideas, today offers opportunities to expand your mind and spirit. Conversations with people from different backgrounds may inspire you, challenging old beliefs and opening you to new possibilities. Say yes to invitations that excite your curiosity, even if they feel unfamiliar. Growth comes from stretching beyond the comfortable. Your curiosity is your compass—follow it.

Affirmation & Gratitude

"I welcome new perspectives and embrace experiences that broaden my horizons."

Gemini
27-April-2026

Career and long-term goals come into sharp focus today. Recognition for your work is possible, or you may feel called to clarify your ambitions. This is a day for planning and strategy rather than rushing ahead. Consider where you want to be in the next few years and align your actions accordingly. Guidance from a mentor or someone in authority may prove invaluable—listen with an open mind. Gemini, your adaptability makes you a natural leader—step forward with confidence.

Affirmation & Gratitude

"I am grateful for clarity in my goals and for opportunities that align with my values."

Gemini

28-April-2026

The cosmos calls you inward today, Gemini. Rest, reflection, and self-care are essential now. While your natural energy often thrives on variety and interaction, your inner world needs attention too. Pay attention to dreams, signs, or gut feelings—they may carry guidance you've been overlooking. This is not the time to rush or push forward. By slowing down and nurturing yourself, you restore balance and open space for inspiration. Trust that progress comes not only from doing, but also from being.

Affirmation & Gratitude

"I honour rest and reflection, knowing they restore clarity and strength."

Gemini
29-April-2026

Fresh, lively energy returns, encouraging self-expression and bold action. Gemini, you may feel inspired to start something new, showcase your talents, or simply enjoy being your authentic self. Your charm and wit make you magnetic today—others are drawn to your energy and ideas. Use this momentum to pursue what excites you most. Don't scatter your focus; instead, channel your enthusiasm into one meaningful direction. The universe supports bold, authentic choices—trust yourself to step forward with courage.

Affirmation & Gratitude

"I celebrate my energy and authenticity, knowing they attract opportunities and growth."

Gemini
30-April-2026

Gemini, today your relationships and partnerships step into the spotlight. The stars encourage you to examine the balance between your needs and the needs of others. Compromise may be required, but that doesn't mean sacrificing your voice—speak with clarity and listen with empathy. Conversations today could bring breakthroughs, especially if you've been avoiding a difficult subject. This is also a beautiful day to celebrate the bonds that uplift you, whether romantic, platonic, or professional. By showing up authentically, you'll strengthen the connections that matter most.

Affirmation & Gratitude

"I am grateful for the honesty and balance that nourish my relationships."

May 2026

Gemini
01-May-2026

Practical matters rise to the surface, Gemini, asking for your focus and attention. While you often prefer spontaneity, today is about building structure through steady effort. Organise your schedule, handle financial details, or commit to a health routine you've been considering. Don't scatter your energy across too many tasks—choose one or two priorities and complete them fully. The sense of accomplishment will lift your spirits. Remember, these small steps are what create the freedom and flexibility you love so much.

Affirmation & Gratitude

"I am thankful for routines and structure that support my long-term wellbeing and goals."

Gemini
02-May-2026

Adventure calls, Gemini, and the cosmos is urging you to explore beyond your usual boundaries. This could come in the form of travel, study, or a conversation that inspires new ideas. Your natural curiosity thrives on variety, and today is rich with opportunities to expand your worldview. Don't dismiss an invitation or opportunity simply because it feels unfamiliar. The unknown holds gifts that your adaptable spirit is more than ready to embrace. Say yes, and let your curiosity lead the way.

Affirmation & Gratitude

"I embrace adventure and welcome new experiences that broaden my perspective."

Gemini
03-May-2026

Career matters and long-term ambitions are in the cosmic spotlight today. Recognition for your efforts may arrive, or you may feel the push to take bold steps toward your goals. This is a day to think strategically: where do you want to go, and what actions will get you there? Gemini, your charm and adaptability make you magnetic in professional spaces—don't be afraid to step into the spotlight. Trust that your unique voice is what makes you stand out.

Affirmation & Gratitude

"I am grateful for clarity in my ambitions and the courage to pursue them."

Gemini
04-May-2026

Gemini, the cosmos encourages rest and reflection today. After a busy stretch, your inner world needs attention. This is not a time to push ahead—it's a time to recharge. Quiet activities such as journaling, meditation, or simply unplugging from the noise will bring you clarity. Subtle insights may rise when you least expect them. Trust that even when you pause, progress is unfolding in the background. Honour your need for balance, and you'll return with renewed focus and energy.

Affirmation & Gratitude

"I honour rest as a vital part of my growth and clarity."

Gemini
05-May-2026

Fresh energy fills the day, lifting your confidence and inspiring bold action. This is the perfect time to express yourself fully, Gemini. Whether through creativity, communication, or leadership, your authenticity shines brightly. Others are drawn to your lively energy, and opportunities may arrive simply because of your openness. Focus your enthusiasm on one meaningful path instead of scattering it across too many ideas. The stars remind you: your uniqueness is your superpower—share it without hesitation.

Affirmation & Gratitude

"I celebrate my individuality and step boldly into opportunities that inspire me."

Gemini
06-May-2026

Gemini, relationships come into focus today, and you may be asked to balance your independence with cooperation. Your natural ability to communicate clearly makes this an excellent time to resolve misunderstandings or share your feelings honestly. Remember, true harmony isn't about avoiding tension—it's about working through it with patience and respect. If you're single, you may encounter someone who piques your interest, perhaps through shared ideas or social settings. If partnered, this is a chance to strengthen trust. Listen as much as you speak, and you'll deepen your bonds.

Affirmation & Gratitude

"I am grateful for relationships that thrive on honesty, respect, and genuine care."

Gemini
07-May-2026

Practical energy surrounds you today, urging you to take care of details that have been lingering on your to-do list. Gemini, while your mind thrives on variety, the cosmos highlights the need for structure and responsibility now. Focus on tasks related to health, finances, or organisation. These small steps will provide stability and free your mind for the creativity you love. Don't scatter your energy across too many things—prioritise what truly matters. By grounding yourself today, you'll feel lighter and more focused tomorrow.

Affirmation & Gratitude

"I am thankful for the structure and discipline that create balance in my life."

Gemini
08-May-2026

Gemini, your adventurous spirit is awakened today, encouraging you to break free from routine. You may feel inspired to learn something new, explore different cultures, or even plan a trip. Conversations with people who hold different beliefs may spark surprising insights. Don't shy away from opportunities that feel unfamiliar—they may be exactly what you need to grow. Trust your curiosity; it will lead you toward expansion and excitement. Today, you're reminded that growth happens when you step into the unknown with courage and openness.

Affirmation & Gratitude

"I welcome adventure and embrace the wisdom new experiences bring."

Gemini
09-May-2026

Your career and long-term ambitions take the spotlight again. Gemini, recognition for your skills is possible, or you may feel the urge to clarify your next steps. This is a day for aligning your actions with your vision. Don't be afraid to think big—your adaptability gives you the tools to pivot as needed. Conversations with mentors or authority figures could provide valuable guidance. Step into opportunities with confidence, but ensure they align with your authentic self. Success will follow when you're true to your own values.

Affirmation & Gratitude

"I am grateful for clarity in my career path and the courage to pursue it."

Gemini
10-May-2026

The stars call you inward today, encouraging rest, reflection, and self-care. Gemini, your busy mind often resists slowing down, but this is where you'll find balance and clarity. Pay attention to your dreams or subtle feelings—your intuition is strong now. This is not a day to force progress but to trust the process unfolding behind the scenes. Allow yourself permission to pause without guilt. When you restore your energy, you'll be ready to move forward with fresh perspective and strength.

Affirmation & Gratitude

"I honour rest as essential, knowing it restores my clarity and focus."

Gemini
11-May-2026

A surge of energy returns, Gemini, filling you with confidence and vitality. Today is ideal for self-expression, creativity, and new beginnings. You may feel called to launch a project, share your ideas, or step into a more visible role. People are drawn to your energy and may be inspired by your enthusiasm. Avoid scattering your focus across too many things—choose one direction that excites you most and commit fully. This is a day to shine brightly and unapologetically.

Affirmation & Gratitude
"I celebrate my individuality and embrace opportunities to shine."

Gemini
12-May-2026

Partnerships take centre stage again today, highlighting balance, cooperation, and honesty. You may need to compromise or work through differences with someone close. Use your natural wit to keep the mood light, but don't avoid important discussions. When you approach conversations with openness and respect, you strengthen the trust that underpins meaningful connections. This is also a beautiful day to appreciate the people who support you and to express gratitude for their role in your journey.

Affirmation & Gratitude

"I am thankful for the love, trust, and respect that nourish my relationships."

Gemini
13-May-2026

Gemini, practical energy fills the day, urging you to focus on health, organisation, and responsibilities. While your curious mind often resists routine, the stars remind you that structure creates freedom. This is a good day to fine-tune your schedule, organise your space, or address financial matters you've been putting off. Don't overwhelm yourself—choose one or two priorities and handle them with focus. By tending to these practical details, you'll clear space for creativity and adventure. Remember, balance comes when you honour both freedom and discipline in your life.

Affirmation & Gratitude

"I am grateful for the balance that steady effort and organisation bring."

Gemini
14-May-2026

Adventure calls, Gemini, and the cosmos encourages you to broaden your horizons. You may feel inspired to learn something new, travel, or dive into conversations that challenge your thinking. Today is about stepping beyond your comfort zone and trusting your curiosity to guide you. Don't be afraid to question old beliefs or routines—this is how growth begins. A chance encounter or idea could spark long-term inspiration. Feed your mind with new experiences, and your spirit will feel alive and renewed.

Affirmation & Gratitude

"I welcome new experiences and embrace the wisdom they bring into my journey."

Gemini
15-May-2026

Gemini, today brings focus to your career and ambitions. Recognition may come your way, or you may feel the urge to refine your goals. The universe is asking you to align your professional path with your authentic values. Success without meaning will not satisfy you—so aim for both. Conversations with mentors, colleagues, or authority figures could shape your direction. Be bold enough to step into the spotlight, but humble enough to learn from feedback. Trust that your adaptability makes you capable of handling opportunities as they arise.

Affirmation & Gratitude

"I am grateful for clarity in my career and the opportunities guiding my growth."

Gemini
16-May-2026

The cosmos encourages rest and inner connection today. Gemini, your lively spirit often thrives on activity, but this is a time to recharge. Pay attention to dreams, intuition, or subtle signs—they may carry guidance you've been overlooking. Reflection can reveal insights that your busy mind has pushed aside. Honour your need for solitude and stillness without guilt; this is how balance is restored. By slowing down, you create the space for clarity, inspiration, and emotional renewal to emerge. Trust that this pause is part of your forward momentum.

Affirmation & Gratitude

"I honour rest and reflection as vital parts of my growth."

Gemini
17-May-2026

Gemini, fresh energy fills your day, sparking confidence and creativity. This is a time to express your individuality and take bold action. Opportunities to showcase your talents or start something new are supported by the stars. Don't hold back—your authenticity is what makes you magnetic. Focus on one project or passion to avoid scattering your energy. You'll find that progress flows easily when you act with courage and purpose. People are drawn to your enthusiasm, so use it to inspire both yourself and others.

Affirmation & Gratitude

"I celebrate my uniqueness and act with confidence and authenticity."

Gemini

18-May-2026

Relationships take the spotlight again, Gemini. Today is about connection, balance, and cooperation. Whether in love, friendship, or professional partnerships, you may find yourself navigating compromise or engaging in heartfelt discussions. Use your natural communication skills to bridge gaps and bring understanding, but don't forget to listen as much as you speak. Honest exchanges can heal misunderstandings and deepen trust. This is also a beautiful day to celebrate the people who uplift and support you on your journey.

Affirmation & Gratitude

"I am thankful for the trust and love that strengthen my relationships."

Gemini
19-May-2026

Practical tasks and routines demand your focus today. Gemini, while your restless spirit prefers variety, the cosmos encourages discipline now. Pay attention to health, organisation, or financial matters. These small actions may feel unexciting but are essential for building long-term stability. Avoid scattering your energy—prioritise what truly matters and commit fully. By grounding yourself in the practical, you create space for more freedom later. Balance is found when you honour both responsibility and exploration. Productivity today will leave you feeling lighter and more in control.

Affirmation & Gratitude

"I am grateful for the discipline that creates balance and stability in my life."

Gemini
20-May-2026

Gemini, adventure calls again, and the stars are urging you to broaden your perspective. This could come through travel, study, or conversations with people who challenge your thinking. Your mind is hungry for new experiences, and today offers opportunities to feed it. Don't shy away from stepping beyond your comfort zone—this is where growth happens. A new idea or connection could open doors that lead to long-term change. Follow your curiosity with courage, and you'll discover inspiration that lights up your path.

Affirmation & Gratitude

"I welcome adventure and trust curiosity to guide me toward growth."

Gemini
21-May-2026

Happy Birthday season begins, Gemini! The Sun enters your sign, bringing a surge of energy, confidence, and possibility. This is your time to shine, step into fresh opportunities, and embrace your individuality. Use this powerful energy to set intentions for the year ahead. What do you truly want to create? Where do you want to grow? The cosmos supports bold new beginnings now, so don't be afraid to dream big. Your natural charm and wit are magnetic—trust yourself to lead with authenticity.

Affirmation & Gratitude

"I celebrate the light within me and embrace new beginnings with joy and courage."

Gemini
22-May-2026

Gemini, today's energy highlights your partnerships and relationships. With the Sun in your sign, you may feel more aware of how others see you. Pay attention to the balance between giving and receiving. Conversations may carry extra weight, offering opportunities to deepen trust or address unresolved issues. Use your natural gift for communication to bridge gaps, but remember to listen as much as you speak. Harmony comes when both sides feel valued. This is a chance to strengthen bonds through honesty and openness.

Affirmation & Gratitude

"I am grateful for relationships built on trust, respect, and mutual care."

Gemini
23-May-2026

Practical responsibilities step into focus today. Gemini, while you love spontaneity, the stars remind you of the value of structure and consistency. Focus on tasks that support your wellbeing—whether through organisation, financial planning, or health routines. Don't let the details overwhelm you; choose one priority and tackle it steadily. This is a day for grounding yourself in routines that provide stability. By attending to these practical matters now, you'll create more freedom and flexibility for the adventures you love.

Affirmation & Gratitude

"I am thankful for routines that create balance, stability, and flow in my life."

Gemini
24-May-2026

Adventure energy rises again, urging you to stretch beyond the familiar. Gemini, this is an ideal day for learning, travel, or exploring new ideas. Conversations may spark inspiration and help you see things from a different perspective. Follow your curiosity—it's your greatest guide right now. Don't be afraid to take a chance on something that feels unfamiliar. Growth is found in the unknown, and today offers opportunities to embrace it. Your adaptable nature makes you ready for what lies ahead.

Affirmation & Gratitude

"I welcome new ideas and experiences that expand my mind and spirit."

Gemini
25-May-2026

Gemini, your career and ambitions come into the spotlight. Recognition for your hard work may arrive, or you may feel compelled to refine your long-term goals. This is a powerful day to consider where you want to be in the years ahead. Align your daily actions with that vision, and you'll build momentum. A mentor or authority figure could provide valuable insights—be open to their guidance. Stand tall in your authenticity, and remember: your originality is what makes your work impactful.

Affirmation & Gratitude

"I am grateful for clarity in my ambitions and for the courage to pursue them."

Gemini
26-May-2026

The cosmos turns your focus inward today, Gemini. After days of outward activity, your spirit needs rest and reflection. This is not a time to push or force progress. Instead, allow stillness to guide you. Dreams, intuition, or subtle signs may reveal the answers you've been seeking. Journaling or meditating can help you connect with these messages. By honouring your need for peace and solitude, you'll return to the world with renewed clarity and strength. Trust that the pause is part of your progress.

Affirmation & Gratitude

"I honour rest and reflection as essential to my growth and clarity."

Gemini
27-May-2026

Gemini, fresh energy fills your day, encouraging you to embrace your individuality and take bold action. With the Sun in your sign, your confidence is glowing, and others are drawn to your charisma and ideas. This is a perfect time to showcase your talents, speak your truth, or begin a project that reflects your authentic self. The key is focus—don't scatter your energy across too many directions. Commit to what excites you most, and you'll see meaningful progress. The universe is supporting bold, authentic moves now.

Affirmation & Gratitude

"I celebrate my uniqueness and take confident steps toward my dreams."

Gemini
28-May-2026

Relationships and partnerships are emphasised today, Gemini. You may find yourself navigating balance, compromise, or heartfelt discussions. Use your gift of communication to foster harmony, but remember that listening is just as powerful as speaking. If you're single, new connections may feel promising. If you're partnered, this is a chance to strengthen bonds through honesty and presence. Avoid skimming the surface; deeper connections require vulnerability and patience. By showing up authentically, you'll nurture trust and intimacy in your relationships.

Affirmation & Gratitude

"I am grateful for relationships that grow stronger through honesty, patience, and love."

Gemini
29-May-2026

Practical responsibilities take priority today, and while they may feel mundane, they are the foundation of your freedom, Gemini. Pay attention to details around work, finances, or health. Tackle one important task instead of scattering your attention across many. This is also a good day to evaluate your habits—are they supporting your energy, or draining it? By fine-tuning your routines, you set yourself up for greater stability in the future. The stars remind you that discipline creates freedom.

Affirmation & Gratitude

"I am thankful for the discipline that builds stability and balance in my life."

Gemini
30-May-2026

Gemini, the cosmos stirs your adventurous spirit today. You may crave variety, exploration, and fresh perspectives. This is an ideal time for study, travel, or conversations with people who challenge you to see the world differently. Inspiration is everywhere if you remain open. Don't shy away from something unfamiliar—it may spark a long-term interest or opportunity. Your curiosity is your greatest gift, and following it will lead to exciting discoveries. Let your mind wander into new territories today—it will feed your spirit.

Affirmation & Gratitude

"I welcome adventure and new ideas that expand my horizons."

Gemini
31-May-2026

Career and long-term ambitions step into the spotlight today. Recognition may arrive, or you may feel a strong urge to refine your goals. This is a day to align action with vision—clarify what success means to you and pursue it authentically. A conversation with a mentor or authority figure could provide valuable insight. Don't underestimate your influence, Gemini—your adaptability and originality are strengths that set you apart. Stand tall in your truth and allow your confidence to shine.

Affirmation & Gratitude

"I am grateful for clarity in my goals and the opportunities guiding me forward."

June 2026

Gemini
01-June-2026

Gemini, today calls for quiet reflection and inner connection. After days of outward focus, your spirit craves stillness. This is a good day to slow down, unplug, and listen to your intuition. Subtle signs may reveal answers you've been searching for. Don't push for clarity—let it emerge naturally. Creative or spiritual practices will feel particularly restorative now. Trust that even in rest, progress is unfolding. The universe often whispers its wisdom in the spaces between action. Honour that pause.

Affirmation & Gratitude

"I honour rest and trust my intuition to reveal the guidance I need."

Gemini
02-June-2026

A wave of fresh energy returns, Gemini, boosting your confidence and inspiring bold self-expression. This is a time to step forward with courage, share your talents, and embrace opportunities that reflect your authenticity. Others notice your sparkle today, and doors may open because of it. Focus on one path that excites you most—scattered energy will dilute your progress. Your adaptability is a gift, but today requires commitment. Choose boldly, and the universe will meet you halfway with support and momentum.

Affirmation & Gratitude

"I celebrate my individuality and trust the universe to support my authentic path."

Gemini
03-June-2026

Gemini, today highlights your relationships, encouraging you to seek balance and harmony. Conversations may carry extra weight, giving you the chance to deepen trust with someone important. Don't shy away from difficult topics —your gift of communication allows you to express yourself clearly and gently. If you're single, new encounters may feel promising. If you're partnered, this is a day to focus on compromise and connection. Remember, strong bonds are built on mutual respect and honesty, not surface-level harmony. Show up authentically, and you'll strengthen the foundation of your partnerships.

Affirmation & Gratitude

"I am grateful for authentic connections built on trust and mutual respect."

Gemini
04-June-2026

The stars draw your attention to routines, health, and responsibilities today. Gemini, while you thrive on variety, the cosmos reminds you of the importance of discipline and structure. Review your habits—are they serving your wellbeing or scattering your energy? Small adjustments can create lasting benefits. This is an ideal day to get organised, tackle a project you've been postponing, or implement a health routine that keeps you energised. Productivity will flow if you approach tasks one at a time. By tending to these practical matters, you create space for future freedom.

Affirmation & Gratitude

"I am thankful for the steady habits that support my wellbeing and balance."

Gemini
05-June-2026

Adventure energy rises, Gemini, sparking your curiosity and love of exploration. You may feel drawn to new ideas, cultures, or studies that broaden your horizons. Don't limit yourself to what's familiar—growth comes when you step into the unknown. Conversations with people who see the world differently may provide inspiration, and travel (even short-distance) could bring refreshing perspective. Your mind is hungry for stimulation today, and the universe is offering it in abundance. Follow the pull of curiosity with an open heart and mind.

Affirmation & Gratitude

"I welcome new perspectives and embrace the growth they bring."

Gemini
06-June-2026

Career and long-term ambitions take centre stage today, Gemini. Recognition for your efforts may come your way, or you may feel inspired to refine your goals. This is a day for strategy and alignment—ensure your daily choices reflect your bigger vision. Mentors or authority figures could provide guidance that shapes your path, so remain open to input. Avoid scattering your focus; concentrate on what feels authentic to your values. Your charm and adaptability make you magnetic in professional spaces—use them wisely to step forward with confidence.

Affirmation & Gratitude

"I am grateful for clarity in my goals and for opportunities that align with my truth."

Gemini
07-June-2026

The cosmos encourages rest and reflection today, Gemini. After recent bursts of activity, your spirit craves stillness. This is not a day for pushing ahead but for allowing space to recharge. Pay attention to your intuition, dreams, or subtle signs—they may carry guidance you've been overlooking. Journaling or meditation will help you process emotions and regain clarity. Trust that pausing is not wasted time—it's essential for balance. By honouring your inner world, you restore energy for the steps ahead.

Affirmation & Gratitude

"I honour the gift of stillness, knowing it restores my clarity and strength."

Gemini
08-June-2026

A wave of fresh energy surrounds you, Gemini, boosting confidence and sparking inspiration. This is a perfect day to take initiative, showcase your talents, or begin a new project. People are drawn to your enthusiasm and adaptability, and opportunities may appear as a result of your lively energy. Focus is key—channel your momentum into one meaningful direction rather than scattering it widely. The stars remind you that bold, authentic action creates ripple effects. Trust yourself to shine brightly and lead with courage.

Affirmation & Gratitude

"I celebrate my individuality and trust my courage to create progress."

Gemini
09-June-2026

Gemini, your relationships are once again in the spotlight, asking you to reflect on balance, trust, and compromise. This is a powerful day to deepen bonds through meaningful conversations. Be open, vulnerable, and willing to listen as much as you share. Avoid skimming over issues with humour—addressing them directly builds stronger connections. If single, you may encounter someone who feels aligned with your values. If partnered, today offers opportunities for growth through mutual honesty and respect. Nurture your connections, and they'll reward you with lasting strength.

Affirmation & Gratitude

"I am grateful for relationships strengthened by honesty, patience, and care."

Gemini
10-June-2026

Gemini, today's energy highlights the practical side of life—work, routines, health, and organisation. While your airy spirit prefers variety, the stars remind you that consistency builds freedom. Take time to streamline your schedule, clear clutter, or establish habits that support your wellbeing. This isn't about perfection; it's about small, steady improvements that create stability. Productivity flows best when you focus on one task at a time instead of scattering your energy. By honouring responsibility today, you set yourself up for more creativity and adventure tomorrow.

Affirmation & Gratitude

"I am thankful for the small steps that bring order, stability, and balance to my life."

Gemini
11-June-2026

Adventure stirs within you today, Gemini, pulling you toward new experiences, knowledge, and perspectives. You may crave travel, a new class, or a deep conversation with someone who thinks differently from you. Feed your restless mind with inspiration, but remember that growth happens when you act on curiosity, not just think about it. Say yes to something unfamiliar—it could open doors to exciting opportunities. The universe is reminding you that your greatest strength is adaptability, and today is about embracing that fully.

Affirmation & Gratitude

"I welcome new ideas and experiences, knowing they expand my horizons."

Gemini
12-June-2026

Gemini, career and public recognition step into the spotlight. This is a day to showcase your skills, share your ideas, or make progress toward your long-term goals. Recognition may come from a mentor, colleague, or authority figure who sees your potential. Be strategic and thoughtful—align your ambitions with your authentic self. Avoid scattering your energy across too many opportunities; instead, focus on the path that feels most meaningful. Your natural charm and adaptability make you magnetic in professional spaces—use them wisely to inspire and lead.

Affirmation & Gratitude

"I am grateful for clarity in my goals and the courage to pursue them authentically."

Gemini
13-June-2026

The cosmos encourages rest and reflection today. Gemini, after recent focus on outer achievements, your inner world needs attention. Slow down and listen to your intuition—your inner voice is strong now. Dreams or subtle signs may bring guidance you've been overlooking. Avoid forcing progress; allow stillness to restore your balance. This is a good day for journaling, meditation, or creative outlets that soothe your spirit. Trust that by pausing now, you're creating the clarity and energy needed for the next phase of growth.

Affirmation & Gratitude

"I honour rest and trust my inner wisdom to guide my journey."

Gemini
14-June-2026

A burst of fresh energy returns, filling you with confidence and vitality. Gemini, today is perfect for bold self-expression, starting something new, or sharing your gifts openly. People are drawn to your light-hearted charm and enthusiasm—don't be surprised if opportunities come your way simply because of your openness. Focus on one clear goal to avoid scattering your energy. Your authenticity is your greatest strength, and the stars are supporting bold, courageous moves now. Step into the spotlight and own your magic.

Affirmation & Gratitude

"I celebrate my individuality and embrace new opportunities with courage."

Gemini
15-June-2026

Relationships and partnerships are in focus today, Gemini. Balance, compromise, and honest communication are key. You may feel called to address an ongoing issue or simply deepen trust with someone close. Don't avoid difficult conversations—your gift for words allows you to approach them with grace. If single, you may attract someone who resonates with your values. If partnered, use today to strengthen your bond through vulnerability and openness. Remember, harmony grows when both sides feel heard and respected.

Affirmation & Gratitude

"I am thankful for the honesty and trust that strengthen my connections."

Gemini
16-June-2026

Practical responsibilities take priority today. Gemini, while your curious mind loves variety, the cosmos asks you to ground yourself in the details. Focus on organisation, health, or financial matters that need your attention. Productivity flows when you handle one task at a time instead of scattering your energy. This is also a good day to refine your routines—small adjustments now will ripple into long-term stability. Balance comes when you honour both freedom and responsibility. Today, discipline becomes your ally, not your burden.

Affirmation & Gratitude

"I am grateful for routines and structure that support my freedom and growth."

Gemini
17-June-2026

Gemini, the stars stir your adventurous spirit today, urging you to seek inspiration beyond the familiar. This is a powerful day for learning, exploring, or connecting with people who broaden your worldview. Conversations may spark fresh insights, or you may feel pulled to study something that excites your curiosity. Don't hold back from stepping outside your routine—growth often comes when you dare to try something new. Travel, even short-distance, could be particularly rewarding now. The universe is inviting you to feed your restless mind with new experiences that energise your soul.

Affirmation & Gratitude

"I welcome new experiences that inspire growth and expand my horizons."

Gemini
18-June-2026

Career matters step into focus again, Gemini, and the cosmos asks you to take your long-term goals seriously. Recognition or new responsibilities may arrive, reminding you of your ability to lead with confidence. You may feel the urge to refine your ambitions, ensuring they align with your authentic values. Authority figures or mentors could provide guidance, so remain open to feedback. This is not a day for scattering your energy—choose one clear direction and move toward it with purpose. Success now is built on both strategy and authenticity.

Affirmation & Gratitude

"I am grateful for clarity in my goals and the courage to pursue them."

Gemini
19-June-2026

The energy today turns inward, calling for reflection and renewal. Gemini, your lively spirit thrives on constant activity, but stillness is just as important. Slow down, listen to your intuition, and let subtle signs guide you. Dreams or flashes of inspiration may reveal truths you've overlooked. This is not the time to push forward but to restore balance. Creative or spiritual practices will feel especially nourishing now. Honour the pause— it allows space for wisdom and clarity to surface naturally. By resting today, you prepare yourself for tomorrow's progress.

Affirmation & Gratitude
"I honour stillness and trust my inner wisdom to guide me."

Gemini
20-June-2026

A burst of vibrant energy returns, Gemini, filling you with confidence and excitement. Today is perfect for self-expression, bold action, and new beginnings. Opportunities may come your way simply because of your lively energy and adaptability. Use this momentum to push forward with something that excites you —whether a creative project, personal goal, or professional step. Focus on what truly lights you up, and avoid scattering your attention too widely. The universe supports courage and authenticity now, so trust your instincts and move boldly.

Affirmation & Gratitude

"I celebrate my individuality and embrace the courage to begin anew."

Gemini
21-June-2026

Relationships take centre stage today, Gemini. Whether romantic, platonic, or professional, the cosmos asks you to focus on balance, cooperation, and honest communication. If there have been misunderstandings, this is the perfect time to clear the air. Your ability to blend humour with honesty makes you a natural peacemaker—use this gift wisely. If single, you may feel drawn to someone who excites your curiosity. If partnered, deeper connection is possible through vulnerability and patience. Today is about giving and receiving love equally.

Affirmation & Gratitude

"I am thankful for the love, trust, and balance in my relationships."

Gemini

22-June-2026

Practical energy takes over, highlighting your routines, health, and responsibilities. Gemini, while you thrive on change, the stars encourage discipline now. This is a good day to refine your schedule, handle details, or commit to wellness practices that support your long-term vitality. Avoid scattering your focus—choose one task at a time and give it your full attention. Productivity flows when you bring order to the small things. By tending to the details, you create a strong foundation that allows freedom and flexibility elsewhere in life.

Affirmation & Gratitude

"I am grateful for the steady habits that support my energy and balance."

Gemini
23-June-2026

Adventure energy rises again, urging you to stretch beyond your familiar comfort zone. Gemini, your restless spirit craves variety, and today is rich with opportunities to explore. This could mean diving into study, having deep conversations, or embracing travel plans. Don't shy away from ideas that challenge your perspective—this is how growth unfolds. Curiosity is your greatest gift, and following it will lead to surprising discoveries. The stars encourage you to say yes to opportunities that expand your world and feed your spirit.

Affirmation & Gratitude

"I embrace new ideas and experiences that expand my heart and mind."

Gemini
24-June-2026

Gemini, today your career and ambitions move into sharp focus. Recognition or an opportunity may arrive that puts you in the spotlight. Don't shy away from stepping into leadership—your quick thinking and adaptability make you well-suited to shine. Reflect on whether your current goals truly align with your deeper values. Success feels most fulfilling when it reflects both achievement and authenticity. Authority figures or mentors could guide you now, so keep your ears open. Strategic planning will give you momentum, so take time to define your path clearly.

Affirmation & Gratitude

"I am grateful for opportunities that align with my values and guide my professional growth."

Gemini
25-June-2026

The cosmos encourages rest and reflection today. Gemini, while you thrive on activity, your inner world also requires attention. Slow down, recharge, and listen to the whispers of your intuition. Dreams, signs, or flashes of insight may reveal truths you've been overlooking. Avoid cramming your schedule with obligations—peace and clarity are your priorities now. This pause will restore balance, preparing you for the fresh energy to come. Trust that even in stillness, growth is happening. Honour the process of resting and allow your inner wisdom to rise to the surface.

Affirmation & Gratitude

"I honour stillness, trusting it restores my clarity, balance, and strength."

Gemini
26-June-2026

A surge of fresh energy arrives, Gemini, filling you with confidence and excitement. Today favours bold self-expression, new beginnings, and stepping forward into opportunities that inspire you. Your charm and lively spirit attract people, making this a good time to share ideas or showcase your talents. Focus on one meaningful direction rather than scattering your energy. Progress is easier now when you commit fully. The stars remind you that authenticity is your greatest strength, so lead with your true self, and success will naturally follow.

Affirmation & Gratitude

"I celebrate my individuality and step forward with courage and joy."

Gemini
27-June-2026

Relationships and partnerships come into focus again today, Gemini. Balance, compromise, and cooperation are highlighted. A heartfelt conversation could strengthen bonds, whether romantic, friendly, or professional. If single, you may feel drawn to someone who sparks your curiosity in unexpected ways. If partnered, today is an opportunity to deepen trust and renew commitment. Your ability to blend humour with honesty makes tough topics easier to navigate—use this gift to your advantage. By showing up authentically, you invite harmony and genuine connection into your life.

Affirmation & Gratitude

"I am thankful for the honesty and love that strengthen my relationships."

Gemini
28-June-2026

Gemini, practical matters and responsibilities take priority today. The stars encourage you to focus on health, finances, or organisation. While you may resist routine, structure is your ally now—it creates the freedom you crave later. Take small, steady steps rather than overwhelming yourself with everything at once. Productivity flows when you choose one important task and see it through to completion. By tending to the practical details of life, you create a solid foundation for your bigger dreams. Discipline today brings stability tomorrow.

Affirmation & Gratitude

"I am grateful for the structure and habits that support my growth and wellbeing."

Gemini
29-June-2026

Adventure calls once more, Gemini, stirring your curiosity and restless spirit. This is a wonderful day for learning, exploring, and engaging with new ideas or cultures. Conversations may open your mind to fresh perspectives, or you may feel inspired to dive into study or travel planning. Don't limit yourself to what's familiar—growth comes when you step boldly into the unknown. Your natural adaptability makes you more than capable of handling the changes new experiences bring. Trust your curiosity; it will lead you to inspiration and expansion.

Affirmation & Gratitude

"I embrace adventure and welcome the wisdom of new experiences."

Gemini
30-June-2026

Gemini, your career and public image take centre stage once again. Recognition may come your way, or you may feel a renewed drive to push forward with long-term goals. This is a day for aligning your actions with your ambitions. Don't scatter your energy; focus on what truly resonates with your values. Guidance from mentors or authority figures could be invaluable, so be open to advice. Your charisma and adaptability are at their peak now—step into opportunities with confidence, and trust that you're building something meaningful.

Affirmation & Gratitude

"I am grateful for clarity in my goals and the courage to pursue them."

July 2026

Gemini
01-July-2026

Gemini, the cosmos encourages reflection today. After a busy stretch, your spirit craves stillness and a chance to process emotions. Pay attention to dreams, intuition, or subtle signs—they may reveal insights you've been overlooking. Don't pressure yourself to produce or perform. Instead, see the value in slowing down and reconnecting with your inner wisdom. A little solitude or creative expression will restore balance. Trust that pausing today allows you to return tomorrow with sharper focus and renewed strength. Honour rest as part of your progress, not a detour.

Affirmation & Gratitude

"I honour rest as a powerful part of my growth and renewal."

Gemini
02-July-2026

Fresh, vibrant energy returns today, filling you with confidence and enthusiasm. Gemini, this is your time to take bold steps forward. Whether in personal goals, career, or creative projects, the universe supports authentic self-expression now. People notice your spark and may be drawn to your ideas or leadership. Don't scatter your energy across too many tasks—focus on what feels most inspiring. Trust that when you act courageously and from the heart, doors will open in your favour. Your originality is your superpower; share it proudly.

Affirmation & Gratitude

"I celebrate my individuality and take bold, authentic steps toward my dreams."

Gemini
03-July-2026

Gemini, relationships and partnerships come to the forefront today. Balance and compromise may be required, but this is an opportunity to strengthen bonds through openness and honesty. Don't avoid important discussions—your ability to communicate with humour and clarity makes it easier to resolve tension. If you're single, this is a favourable day for meeting someone through shared interests. If partnered, you may feel closer by addressing concerns directly and celebrating what you value together. Connection deepens when both sides feel seen and respected.

Affirmation & Gratitude

"I am grateful for relationships that thrive on honesty, balance, and mutual respect."

Gemini
04-July-2026

Practical responsibilities require your focus, Gemini. Today is about grounding yourself in tasks that bring order to your life—whether finances, health, or organisation. While you prefer variety, the stars remind you that structure provides the freedom you crave. Focus on one priority and see it through; you'll feel lighter and more in control afterward. This is also a good day to review your daily routines and make small adjustments that improve balance. By tending to the details, you create a strong foundation for bigger opportunities.

Affirmation & Gratitude

"I am thankful for the structure and balance that steady effort brings."

Gemini
05-July-2026

The adventurous energy of the cosmos sparks your curiosity today. Gemini, your restless mind craves new ideas, learning, and exploration. This is the perfect time for travel, study, or conversations that inspire fresh perspectives. Don't shy away from something unfamiliar—it may open doors you didn't know existed. Feed your curiosity and allow yourself to stretch beyond routine. You'll discover that growth often comes from saying yes to the unknown. Inspiration is everywhere today—stay open, and you'll find it.

Affirmation & Gratitude

"I welcome new adventures and the wisdom they bring into my life."

Gemini
06-July-2026

Gemini, your career and ambitions step into the spotlight. Recognition or a new opportunity may arrive, or you may feel clarity about your long-term goals. Take this chance to assess whether your daily actions align with your bigger vision. Mentors or authority figures could offer valuable advice, so keep an open mind. Don't scatter your efforts—focus on the path that feels most authentic to you. Your adaptability makes you capable of navigating opportunities, but success comes when you commit with purpose.

Affirmation & Gratitude

"I am grateful for clarity in my ambitions and the courage to act on them."

Gemini
07-July-2026

Today the cosmos calls you inward, encouraging reflection and rest. Gemini, you often thrive in movement and chatter, but quiet moments are equally valuable. Pay attention to dreams, inner nudges, or flashes of intuition—they may reveal guidance about your next steps. Avoid cramming your schedule; instead, give yourself permission to pause. This is a perfect day for meditation, journaling, or creative practices that soothe your spirit. Trust that by resting today, you are refuelling for tomorrow's progress. Balance comes from honouring both your inner and outer worlds.

Affirmation & Gratitude

"I trust my inner wisdom and honour the peace reflection brings."

Gemini
08-July-2026

Gemini, fresh energy returns today, filling you with courage, vitality, and motivation. This is the perfect time to start something new or push ahead with a project that excites you. Your confidence is magnetic, and others may be drawn to your enthusiasm. Avoid scattering your focus across too many directions—choose one path and give it your full attention. Trust your instincts; the universe is supporting authentic moves now. By stepping into your individuality, you inspire others as well as yourself. Your originality is your greatest strength—let it shine without hesitation.

Affirmation & Gratitude

"I celebrate my unique energy and take bold steps toward my goals."

Gemini
09-July-2026

Relationships and partnerships take centre stage today, Gemini. The stars encourage you to balance independence with cooperation. You may need to compromise, listen more deeply, or share honestly about your needs. Use your natural humour and charm to ease tension, but don't shy away from meaningful conversations. If single, this could be a day of promising connections. If partnered, today offers opportunities for closeness and trust. Authenticity matters most—show up fully, and you'll strengthen the bonds that matter most.

Affirmation & Gratitude

"I am grateful for the honesty and balance that nurture my relationships."

Gemini
10-July-2026

Gemini, today highlights routines, health, and practical responsibilities. While your adaptable nature prefers variety, the stars remind you that structure creates freedom. Take time to refine your habits, organise your space, or handle tasks you've been postponing. Productivity flows more easily when you focus on one thing at a time instead of juggling everything at once. Small, consistent efforts made today will ripple into long-term stability and peace of mind. By grounding yourself now, you free your energy for bigger pursuits later.

Affirmation & Gratitude

"I am thankful for the habits that bring balance, health, and stability to my life."

Gemini
11-July-2026

Adventure calls once again, Gemini, sparking your curiosity and desire for growth. This is an ideal day for learning, travel, or connecting with people who broaden your perspective. Don't limit yourself to what feels safe or familiar—the unknown holds opportunities for growth and inspiration. A new idea or conversation may spark a long-term interest. Feed your mind with experiences that excite you, and you'll feel energised and renewed. Your curiosity is your compass today—follow where it leads.

Affirmation & Gratitude
"I welcome new experiences and trust the wisdom they bring into my journey."

Gemini
12-July-2026

Career and ambitions are highlighted today, Gemini. Recognition may come your way, or you may feel motivated to refine your long-term goals. Use this energy to align your daily actions with your bigger vision. Don't be afraid to step into the spotlight—your adaptability and communication skills make you stand out. Seek guidance from mentors or trusted allies; their perspective may prove invaluable. Remember, true success is achieved when it aligns with your authentic self. Pursue what feels meaningful, and your progress will have lasting impact.

Affirmation & Gratitude

"I am grateful for clarity in my career and the courage to pursue it."

Gemini
13-July-2026

The cosmos calls you inward today, Gemini, encouraging rest and reflection. After a busy period, your spirit craves stillness. Pay attention to dreams or intuitive nudges—they may reveal truths you've been overlooking. This is a day for meditation, journaling, or quiet creative outlets. Avoid filling your schedule with unnecessary activity. Honour your inner world, and you'll restore balance for the days ahead. Trust that slowing down is not a setback—it's an essential part of your journey toward clarity and renewal.

Affirmation & Gratitude

"I honour rest and trust my intuition to guide me forward."

Gemini
14-July-2026

A burst of fresh energy returns, Gemini, inspiring bold self-expression and confidence. Today favours taking initiative, starting projects, or showcasing your talents. People notice your lively energy, and opportunities may arrive as a result of your openness and charm. Don't scatter your efforts—focus on one clear path where you can make meaningful progress. The stars remind you that your individuality is your power. By stepping into your authentic self and acting with courage, you set momentum for success.

Affirmation & Gratitude

"I celebrate my individuality and act with confidence and joy."

Gemini
15-July-2026

Gemini, relationships take centre stage today, asking you to focus on balance, trust, and open communication. Whether romantic, platonic, or professional, you may need to compromise or actively listen to ensure harmony. Use your natural gift for humour and conversation to ease tension, but don't avoid deeper truths—addressing them strengthens trust. If single, you may notice a spark with someone who shares your curiosity. If partnered, it's a good day to realign goals together. The stars remind you that partnerships thrive when authenticity and patience walk hand in hand.

Affirmation & Gratitude

"I am grateful for relationships built on honesty, trust, and genuine care."

Gemini
16-July-2026

Gemini, the cosmos draws your focus toward routines, health, and organisation. While your restless mind often resists structure, today you'll benefit from grounding yourself. Small adjustments—whether decluttering your space, revising your schedule, or caring for your body—will have lasting benefits. Productivity comes easily if you avoid multitasking and commit to one task at a time. Think of today as fine-tuning the foundation that supports your freedom. By honouring these details, you give yourself the flexibility and energy to explore bigger dreams later.

Affirmation & Gratitude

"I am thankful for the structure that creates balance and supports my wellbeing."

Gemini
17-July-2026

Adventure is calling, Gemini, and the stars encourage you to step outside your comfort zone. This may come through travel, study, or engaging with people who broaden your perspective. Inspiration arrives when you immerse yourself in something new. Don't hesitate to explore ideas that challenge your current beliefs—this is how growth unfolds. The universe is reminding you that curiosity is your compass. Follow it boldly, and you'll uncover opportunities that awaken your spirit and expand your world in surprising ways.

Affirmation & Gratitude

"I welcome new experiences and embrace the wisdom they bring."

Gemini
18-July-2026

Career and ambitions rise to the surface today, Gemini. Recognition for your efforts may come, or you may feel the push to clarify your long-term direction. Take time to assess whether your actions align with your authentic goals. Mentors or authority figures could provide guidance—be open to their input. You don't need to rush; focus on steady, strategic steps. Your adaptability and quick thinking make you well-suited to navigate opportunities now. Stand tall in your confidence and trust your unique approach.

Affirmation & Gratitude

"I am grateful for clarity in my career and the courage to pursue my path."

Gemini
19-July-2026

The cosmos calls for stillness today, Gemini. Reflection, rest, and inner connection are key. Avoid cramming your schedule with activity; instead, prioritise peace. Intuition is heightened, and subtle insights may appear through dreams or quiet contemplation. By pausing, you give your mind and spirit space to breathe, process, and refocus. Creative or spiritual practices will feel particularly nourishing now. Trust that slowing down restores balance and helps you prepare for fresh momentum ahead. Remember, growth happens in both action and rest.

Affirmation & Gratitude

"I honour rest and reflection as essential parts of my journey."

Gemini
20-July-2026

A surge of vibrant energy fills your day, Gemini. This is a time for confidence, bold action, and self-expression. Share your ideas, showcase your talents, or begin a project that excites you. People are drawn to your energy, and opportunities may arise simply because of your authenticity. The stars remind you to focus on one direction instead of scattering your energy across too many pursuits. By acting with courage and purpose, you create momentum that carries you forward. Step into your individuality—it's your greatest strength.

Affirmation & Gratitude

"I celebrate my individuality and step forward with courage and authenticity."

Gemini
21-July-2026

Relationships and partnerships are in focus again today. Gemini, you may find yourself navigating balance between independence and cooperation. Honest conversations will bring clarity and strengthen bonds. If you've been avoiding an issue, now is the time to address it with patience and empathy. Your charm and quick wit can ease tension, but depth is required for lasting harmony. Single Geminis may attract someone through meaningful exchanges. Today, connection is about authenticity, not performance—show up fully, and love will meet you there.

Affirmation & Gratitude

"I am grateful for authentic connections that nurture love, trust, and balance."

Gemini
22-July-2026

Gemini, today the cosmos highlights your daily routines, health, and responsibilities. While you prefer variety and freedom, the stars remind you that structure creates the space to thrive. This is a perfect time to review your habits—are they energising or draining you? Focus on small, consistent changes like meal planning, exercise, or refining your schedule. Productivity flows when you approach tasks one at a time instead of juggling everything at once. By grounding yourself today, you prepare for bigger adventures tomorrow. Balance between discipline and flexibility is your key to success.

Affirmation & Gratitude

"I am grateful for habits that support my balance, health, and future growth."

Gemini
23-July-2026

Adventure calls strongly today, Gemini. Your curiosity is buzzing, and the universe is nudging you to explore beyond your comfort zone. This could involve learning, travel, or diving into conversations with people who inspire you. Don't be afraid to stretch into unfamiliar territory—it's here that you'll find growth and renewal. A new perspective or experience could spark ideas that shape your next steps in life. Say yes to opportunities that ignite your spirit. The world feels wide open today, and your adaptability makes you ready for the ride.

Affirmation & Gratitude

"I welcome new experiences and the wisdom they bring into my journey."

Gemini
24-July-2026

Gemini, your career and ambitions take centre stage once more. Recognition or an opportunity to showcase your talents may appear, reminding you of your ability to shine. Use this energy to set clear intentions for the future. Align your goals with your values to ensure your path feels meaningful as well as successful. Mentors or colleagues may play a significant role—listen closely to their input. You don't need to rush; steady, thoughtful steps will take you further than impulsive moves. Authenticity and strategy are your allies today.

Affirmation & Gratitude

"I am grateful for clarity in my goals and the courage to pursue them."

Gemini
25-July-2026

The cosmos calls you inward, encouraging reflection and rest. Gemini, while your lively spirit enjoys constant stimulation, today is about slowing down. Honour your inner world with quiet time, journaling, or simply being still. Pay attention to intuition and subtle nudges—they may hold the answers you've been searching for. By stepping away from external noise, you give yourself the gift of clarity. Trust that stillness is part of progress, not a pause from it. Balance comes when you honour both your inner and outer worlds equally.

Affirmation & Gratitude

"I honour rest and reflection, knowing they restore my balance and strength."

Gemini
26-July-2026

A surge of vibrant energy arrives, Gemini, giving you confidence and motivation. This is an excellent day to begin something new, showcase your individuality, or push forward with a project. Your charisma is magnetic, and others may be drawn to your enthusiasm and ideas. The key is focus—don't scatter your energy in too many directions. By committing to one inspired path, you'll create meaningful progress. The universe is supporting bold, authentic action now. Trust yourself to step into opportunities that feel exciting and true to your spirit.

Affirmation & Gratitude

"I celebrate my individuality and embrace bold new beginnings with courage."

Gemini

27-July-2026

Gemini, today relationships and partnerships take centre stage again. Whether in love, friendship, or business, balance and cooperation are highlighted. Open, honest communication will be essential, and your natural gift for words can help bridge any gaps. Don't avoid uncomfortable topics—addressing them with patience will deepen trust. If single, new connections may feel promising. If partnered, this is a chance to strengthen commitment and mutual understanding. The stars remind you that partnerships thrive when both sides feel heard and respected.

Affirmation & Gratitude

"I am grateful for relationships built on honesty, trust, and shared respect."

Gemini
28-July-2026

Practical responsibilities rise to the surface today, Gemini. Focus on health, organisation, or financial matters that require attention. While your mind prefers variety, grounding yourself now will provide lasting benefits. Don't overwhelm yourself with too much at once—prioritise one or two tasks and follow through. These small but consistent efforts are what create stability and peace of mind. By tending to these foundations, you'll free your energy for the creativity and exploration you love. Discipline is your ally today, helping you create balance.

Affirmation & Gratitude

"I am thankful for routines and structure that support my long-term wellbeing."

Gemini
29-July-2026

Gemini, adventure stirs your spirit today. The stars encourage you to explore beyond the boundaries of routine, whether through travel, study, or deep conversations that challenge your thinking. Your mind craves stimulation, and fresh perspectives will fuel your creativity. Don't shy away from opportunities that feel unfamiliar—they may open doors to long-term growth. This is a day to follow your curiosity with courage. By saying yes to exploration, you not only expand your knowledge but also uncover hidden aspects of yourself that bring renewed energy and purpose.

Affirmation & Gratitude

"I welcome new adventures that expand my mind, heart, and soul."

Gemini
30-July-2026

Gemini, career and ambitions rise into focus once more. Recognition may arrive, or you may feel compelled to clarify your long-term goals. This is a time to evaluate whether your current path aligns with your true values. If not, adjustments will bring you closer to authentic success. Guidance from mentors or colleagues could be especially valuable now, so remain open. Avoid scattering your energy; choose one direction that excites you and commit to it fully. With steady effort, the momentum you create today can ripple far into the future.

Affirmation & Gratitude

"I am grateful for clarity in my goals and the courage to pursue them authentically."

Gemini
31-July-2026

The cosmos calls you inward, Gemini, reminding you to balance outer ambition with inner peace. After recent progress, your spirit may crave quiet and stillness. Take time to rest, meditate, or reflect on where you are emotionally. Intuition is heightened today—listen closely to the whispers of your inner voice. Answers may come through dreams, creative expression, or simple moments of silence. Don't push yourself too hard. Trust that slowing down helps you regain balance and clarity, allowing you to move forward with renewed strength.

Affirmation & Gratitude

"I honour stillness and trust the guidance my inner wisdom provides."

August 2026

Gemini
01-August-2026

Gemini, fresh energy surrounds you, encouraging bold self-expression and new beginnings. The stars support you in stepping into your individuality and sharing your talents with the world. Your confidence is magnetic, and opportunities may arise as a result of your authentic presence. Focus on one inspired path rather than scattering your energy across too many ideas. This is the perfect day to start something that feels aligned with your passions. The universe is encouraging you to act courageously, trusting that your originality will open doors.

Affirmation & Gratitude

"I celebrate my individuality and embrace new opportunities with courage and joy."

Gemini
02-August-2026

Relationships are highlighted today, Gemini, and you may find yourself navigating balance, compromise, or heartfelt conversations. Use your gift for communication to express yourself clearly, but remember that listening is equally important. Authentic exchanges will strengthen bonds, whether with a partner, friend, or colleague. If single, you may meet someone who sparks your curiosity. If partnered, use this day to reconnect and reaffirm your shared goals. Harmony thrives when both sides feel valued. Be patient and open—it will bring you closer together.

Affirmation & Gratitude

"I am thankful for the love and balance that enrich my relationships."

Gemini
03-August-2026

Gemini, practical matters and responsibilities take precedence today. While you prefer variety and change, the cosmos reminds you of the importance of structure. Tidy your space, refine your schedule, or pay attention to your health. Even small adjustments will improve balance. Productivity flows when you avoid multitasking and give your focus to one task at a time. Think of today as maintenance work for your life—it may feel small, but it creates long-term stability and peace. By grounding yourself today, you'll feel more free tomorrow.

Affirmation & Gratitude

"I am grateful for the structure and habits that support my growth and wellbeing."

Gemini
04-August-2026

Adventure energy returns, Gemini, inspiring you to explore, learn, and expand your horizons. This could come through travel, study, or engaging with people who see the world differently than you. Your curiosity is your compass, and following it today may reveal exciting new opportunities. Don't dismiss something unfamiliar—it may lead to growth and inspiration you didn't expect. Feed your mind with fresh ideas and your spirit with new experiences. The stars remind you that stepping into the unknown often brings the greatest rewards.

Affirmation & Gratitude

"I welcome new experiences that inspire growth and enrich my journey."

Gemini
05-August-2026

Gemini, your career and ambitions take the spotlight today. Recognition may come from authority figures, colleagues, or through your own sense of accomplishment. The stars encourage you to think strategically—are your current actions moving you toward your long-term goals? If not, this is a good time to adjust course. Mentors or influential people may provide insights that shape your path. Avoid scattering your energy across too many projects. Focus on what feels most aligned with your authentic self, and you'll find momentum building. Success now is grounded in both vision and steady effort.

Affirmation & Gratitude

"I am grateful for clarity in my ambitions and for the guidance that shapes my path."

Gemini
06-August-2026

The cosmos invites you inward today, Gemini, urging rest, reflection, and self-care. Your busy mind thrives on constant stimulation, but balance comes when you also honour stillness. Pay attention to your intuition and dreams—they may carry messages you've been overlooking. Avoid overloading your schedule. This is a perfect day for meditation, journaling, or creative practices that soothe your spirit. Trust that progress is still happening behind the scenes, even if you pause. By creating space, you allow clarity and inspiration to rise naturally.

Affirmation & Gratitude

"I honour stillness as an essential part of balance, clarity, and growth."

Gemini
07-August-2026

A surge of fresh energy returns, Gemini, sparking confidence and bold self-expression. This is a day to step forward, showcase your individuality, and take action on something meaningful. Your charm and wit are magnetic, and others are drawn to your enthusiasm. Don't scatter your energy across too many ideas; instead, channel it into one direction where you can make real progress. Opportunities may arise unexpectedly, so remain open and adaptable. The stars support courage and authenticity now—trust yourself to shine.

Affirmation & Gratitude

"I celebrate my uniqueness and take bold steps that align with my true self."

Gemini
08-August-2026

Relationships and partnerships are emphasised today, Gemini. Balance and compromise are key themes. Whether in love, friendship, or business, you may need to work through differences with honesty and patience. Avoid brushing aside deeper issues with humour—addressing them openly will strengthen bonds. If you're single, this is a favourable time for meaningful encounters. If partnered, today supports deeper trust and understanding. Remember, harmony is built not on perfection, but on authenticity, respect, and a willingness to meet in the middle.

Affirmation & Gratitude

"I am thankful for the balance, respect, and love that nurture my connections."

Gemini
09-August-2026

Gemini, practical matters rise to the surface today. While your mind craves variety, the stars encourage you to ground yourself in routines and responsibilities. Focus on health, organisation, or financial details. Productivity flows when you simplify and focus on one task at a time instead of juggling too much. These small but consistent efforts create long-term stability and ease. Think of today as fine-tuning the structures that support your creativity and freedom. Balance between responsibility and exploration ensures your energy flows smoothly.

Affirmation & Gratitude

"I am grateful for the structure and steady habits that support my wellbeing."

Gemini
10-August-2026

Adventure energy stirs once more, Gemini, filling you with curiosity and restlessness. This is a great day to break from routine and explore new ideas or experiences. Travel, study, or conversations with people from different backgrounds could inspire you in unexpected ways. Don't hesitate to try something unfamiliar—the growth you seek often lies beyond your comfort zone. Your adaptability makes you well-prepared for whatever comes. Feed your spirit with fresh inspiration, and you'll find new perspectives that energise your path forward.

Affirmation & Gratitude

"I welcome adventure and embrace the wisdom of new experiences."

Gemini

11-August-2026

Career and long-term ambitions come into sharp focus today. Recognition is possible, or you may feel strongly motivated to refine your path. Think carefully about what success means to you, Gemini—it's not just about achievements, but about living in alignment with your values. Strategic planning will bring clarity, and support from mentors or colleagues could guide you in the right direction. This is a day to take responsibility for your direction and step forward with confidence. Authenticity will ensure your success is lasting and meaningful.

Affirmation & Gratitude

"I am grateful for clarity in my goals and the confidence to pursue them with integrity."

Gemini
12-August-2026

Gemini, the cosmos invites you to slow down and turn inward. After days of forward momentum, your body and spirit need time to rest and recharge. This is not a day for pushing hard; instead, lean into quiet reflection, meditation, or creative outlets that soothe your soul. Intuition is heightened—listen closely to the whispers within. You may uncover insights about your next steps simply by allowing yourself space. Trust that pausing does not mean losing progress. It restores balance and prepares you for what's coming. Honour the wisdom that stillness brings.

Affirmation & Gratitude

"I honour rest and reflection, trusting they restore balance and clarity."

Gemini
13-August-2026

Fresh, vibrant energy flows back into your life today, Gemini. Confidence is high, and the stars encourage you to embrace self-expression and bold action. This is an excellent day to begin a new project, share your ideas, or simply celebrate your individuality. People are drawn to your magnetic energy, and opportunities may arrive because of it. Avoid scattering your focus across too many directions—choose one inspired path and pour your energy into it. Authenticity is your greatest strength; let it guide your choices today.

Affirmation & Gratitude
"I celebrate my individuality and courageously step into new opportunities."

Gemini
14-August-2026

Relationships and partnerships are highlighted today. Gemini, you may feel called to nurture balance, compromise, and cooperation. If there's been tension, use your natural humour and communication skills to ease the atmosphere, but don't avoid important discussions. Harmony grows when honesty and vulnerability are present. Single Geminis may meet someone intriguing, while those partnered can deepen trust through openness. Remember, connections thrive when both sides feel valued and respected. Show up authentically, and you'll strengthen the bonds that matter most.

Affirmation & Gratitude

"I am grateful for the honesty and respect that deepen my connections."

Gemini
15-August-2026

Practical responsibilities come into play today, Gemini. While your adaptable nature prefers variety, the stars remind you of the importance of consistency. Focus on tasks related to work, finances, or health. Approach them step by step instead of overwhelming yourself with everything at once. Productivity will flow if you simplify your priorities. By tending to the small details, you create a strong foundation for your freedom and creativity. Think of today as maintenance work for your dreams—necessary and rewarding in the long run.

Affirmation & Gratitude
"I am thankful for the routines that support balance, stability, and growth."

Gemini
16-August-2026

Gemini, adventure energy rises again, filling you with curiosity and restlessness. This is a great day to explore, whether through travel, study, or meaningful conversations with people outside your usual circle. Fresh perspectives will spark inspiration, and the universe encourages you to follow your curiosity. Don't shy away from the unfamiliar—it could open doors to long-term opportunities. Your mind thrives when engaged with new ideas, and today offers plenty. Say yes to what excites your spirit, and let exploration guide you.

Affirmation & Gratitude

"I welcome new experiences and the growth they bring into my life."

Gemini
17-August-2026

Career and ambitions take centre stage once more, Gemini. Recognition for your work may arrive, or you may feel clarity about your long-term goals. The stars encourage you to align your professional path with your authentic self. Mentors, authority figures, or colleagues could provide valuable input—listen closely to their advice. Avoid scattering your energy across too many opportunities. Focus on what feels most meaningful and sustainable. Success now is about balance: achieving results while staying true to your values and passions.

Affirmation & Gratitude

"I am grateful for clarity in my ambitions and the courage to pursue them authentically."

Gemini
18-August-2026

The cosmos calls you inward again, reminding you of the importance of stillness and reflection. Gemini, while you thrive on activity and variety, balance requires quiet moments too. Pay attention to dreams, gut feelings, or signs—they may reveal truths you've been overlooking. Avoid rushing or forcing clarity; instead, create space for insights to flow naturally. Today is best spent restoring your energy through solitude, journaling, or gentle self-care. Trust that the pause is not wasted time—it's part of your growth. Honour your inner world with patience.

Affirmation & Gratitude

"I trust the wisdom of stillness and honour my need for rest and clarity."

Gemini
19-August-2026

Gemini, a wave of fresh energy arrives today, encouraging bold self-expression and confidence. This is your chance to showcase your talents, take initiative, and pursue something meaningful. Others are drawn to your natural charm and adaptability, so opportunities may come simply because of your openness. Focus your energy carefully—avoid scattering it across too many projects. By committing to one inspired path, you'll make real progress. The stars remind you that authenticity is your greatest strength, and leading with it brings fulfilment and recognition. Shine brightly today—your individuality is your superpower.

Affirmation & Gratitude

"I celebrate my individuality and take confident steps toward my dreams."

Gemini
20-August-2026

Relationships and partnerships step into the spotlight today, Gemini. Whether in love, friendship, or business, balance and cooperation are key. You may need to compromise, listen more deeply, or address an unresolved issue. Your gift for communication allows you to bridge gaps and create harmony, but remember that listening is as important as speaking. If single, new connections may feel promising. If partnered, today offers opportunities to deepen trust and reaffirm your bond. Authenticity and patience will nurture stronger, lasting connections.

Affirmation & Gratitude

"I am grateful for the honesty and balance that strengthen my relationships."

Gemini

21-August-2026

Gemini, practical responsibilities come into focus. The cosmos asks you to ground yourself in routines, health, and organisation. While your curious spirit craves variety, today is about building stability through consistent effort. Tackle lingering tasks, tidy your space, or refine your schedule. Avoid multitasking; focus on one important priority and complete it fully. These small but steady steps create balance and support your freedom in the long run. Productivity feels satisfying today, reminding you that discipline and flexibility can work hand in hand.

Affirmation & Gratitude

"I am thankful for routines and steady habits that support my balance and growth."

Gemini

22-August-2026

Adventure beckons once again, Gemini, stirring your curiosity and restlessness. This is a day for exploration—whether through travel, study, or engaging with people who inspire new perspectives. Say yes to opportunities that stretch your mind and spirit, even if they feel unfamiliar. The universe is reminding you that growth happens beyond your comfort zone. A conversation or experience today could spark ideas that shape your path forward. Trust your adaptability; it's your greatest ally in navigating the unknown with ease and excitement.

Affirmation & Gratitude

"I welcome new experiences and trust they bring wisdom and inspiration."

Gemini
23-August-2026

Career and ambitions are highlighted today. Recognition may come for past efforts, or new opportunities may appear that align with your long-term vision. Take time to reflect on what success truly means to you—it's not only about achievement, but about alignment with your values. Mentors or authority figures may guide you with insights that prove invaluable. Focus on strategy rather than rushing forward impulsively. When you align your authenticity with your goals, success flows more naturally. This is a day to step forward confidently and trust your direction.

Affirmation & Gratitude

"I am grateful for clarity in my ambitions and the courage to pursue them authentically."

Gemini
24-August-2026

The cosmos invites you to slow down today, Gemini. After recent progress, your body and mind crave reflection and rest. Pay attention to subtle signs, dreams, or gut feelings—they may reveal guidance you've been overlooking. Avoid cramming your schedule with too many obligations; instead, allow stillness to bring clarity. Creative or spiritual practices are especially nourishing now. Trust that pausing is not a setback—it restores balance and prepares you for fresh momentum. By honouring your inner world today, you set the stage for tomorrow's success.

Affirmation & Gratitude

"I honour rest and trust the clarity it brings into my journey."

Gemini

25-August-2026

A burst of vibrant energy returns, Gemini, lifting your spirit and sparking confidence. Today is ideal for self-expression, new beginnings, or pushing forward with something meaningful. Your charisma and adaptability attract attention, making this a powerful time to showcase your talents or share your ideas. Don't spread yourself too thin—choose one inspired path and pour your energy into it. Authenticity is your key to progress now. The stars encourage you to step boldly into the spotlight and let your individuality guide you.

Affirmation & Gratitude

"I celebrate my uniqueness and step forward with courage and joy."

Gemini
26-August-2026

Gemini, relationships are highlighted today, drawing your focus toward balance and connection. Whether in romance, friendship, or professional partnerships, the stars encourage honest communication and cooperation. Use your natural wit to lighten the mood, but don't avoid deeper conversations—facing them builds trust. If you're single, you may feel sparks with someone who shares your intellectual curiosity. If you're partnered, this is a great day to reaffirm shared goals and strengthen your bond. Remember, authentic connection requires both listening and speaking with care.

Affirmation & Gratitude

"I am grateful for relationships that grow stronger through honesty and trust."

Gemini
27-August-2026

Practical responsibilities rise to the surface, Gemini, and the cosmos encourages you to ground yourself. Health, organisation, and routine may demand your attention. While you often resist structure, today it will bring a sense of accomplishment and balance. Focus on the details—tidy your space, review finances, or create a schedule that supports your goals. Avoid multitasking; productivity flows when you focus on one task at a time. By handling these small steps now, you create the foundation that supports your adventurous spirit later.

Affirmation & Gratitude
"I am thankful for the structure that brings balance and freedom to my life."

Gemini

28-August-2026

Gemini, your adventurous side awakens again, and the stars encourage exploration. This could take the form of travel, study, or meaningful conversations that inspire fresh insights. Curiosity is your greatest strength—follow it today with an open mind. Don't dismiss new ideas simply because they're unfamiliar; they may spark growth and opportunity. Stepping outside your comfort zone may feel uncertain at first, but it leads to expansion and joy. Feed your restless mind with inspiration, and you'll feel renewed and re-energised.

Affirmation & Gratitude

"I welcome new perspectives and embrace the wisdom they bring."

Gemini

29-August-2026

Career and ambitions take centre stage, Gemini. Recognition for your work may appear, or you may feel motivated to refine your long-term goals. This is a day to think strategically and align your daily actions with your bigger vision. Don't scatter your energy across too many pursuits—focus on the direction that feels most authentic to you. Guidance from a mentor or authority figure could help shape your path. Stand tall in your confidence and trust your adaptability—it makes you ready to seize opportunities as they come.

Affirmation & Gratitude

"I am grateful for clarity in my goals and the courage to pursue them authentically."

Gemini
30-August-2026

The cosmos turns your focus inward, Gemini, encouraging rest, reflection, and reconnection with your inner world. After recent busyness, this is your time to pause and recharge. Listen closely to your intuition—subtle insights may provide guidance you've been overlooking. Don't overload yourself with obligations; prioritise peace and stillness. Journaling, meditation, or creative expression will feel especially nourishing. Trust that slowing down is not wasted time—it's a crucial part of progress. Honour your inner needs, and you'll return with clarity and renewed energy.

Affirmation & Gratitude

"I honour stillness and trust my inner wisdom to guide me."

Gemini
31-August-2026

A fresh surge of energy surrounds you today, Gemini, boosting your confidence and creativity. This is the perfect time to step into self-expression and embrace new beginnings. People are drawn to your authenticity, and opportunities may arrive simply because of your openness. Focus your enthusiasm rather than scattering it—commit to what excites you most. Bold action taken now will have lasting ripple effects. The stars remind you that your individuality is your strength, and sharing it will inspire others as much as yourself.

Affirmation & Gratitude

"I celebrate my uniqueness and take bold steps toward my dreams."

September 2026

Gemini
01-September-2026

Gemini, relationships come into focus again today. This is a day for balance, cooperation, and honest communication. Whether in love, friendship, or business, you may need to compromise or share your perspective openly. Avoid glossing over issues—authentic conversations bring healing and deeper connection. If single, you may feel drawn to someone who mirrors your curiosity and humour. If partnered, today is an opportunity to realign and strengthen your bond. Remember, meaningful partnerships grow when both sides feel heard, respected, and valued.

Affirmation & Gratitude

"I am grateful for connections built on honesty, balance, and mutual respect."

Gemini

02-September-2026

Gemini, the cosmos directs your attention toward practical responsibilities. While your curious mind prefers variety, today is about focusing on structure, organisation, and wellbeing. Take time to refine your routines, handle financial details, or prioritise your health. Productivity flows when you avoid multitasking and dedicate yourself to one task at a time. These small, steady steps may not feel glamorous, but they create long-term stability and peace of mind. Think of today as building a foundation strong enough to support your adventures. By honouring discipline, you'll unlock greater freedom later.

Affirmation & Gratitude

"I am thankful for the steady habits that bring balance, health, and stability."

Gemini
03-September-2026

Adventure energy rises, Gemini, filling you with curiosity and excitement. This is a perfect day to step outside your comfort zone, whether through travel, study, or conversations that challenge your thinking. New perspectives could spark insights that shift the way you see your path forward. Don't hold back from saying yes to opportunities, even if they feel unfamiliar—you are well-equipped to handle change. Your adaptability is your gift, and the universe is rewarding your willingness to explore. Growth and inspiration are waiting for you in the unknown.

Affirmation & Gratitude
"I welcome new perspectives and embrace the wisdom they bring into my life."

Gemini

04-September-2026

Gemini, your career and ambitions take centre stage again today. Recognition for past efforts may come, or you may feel the push to refine your goals with greater clarity. Align your professional path with your authentic values—success feels most satisfying when it reflects your true self. Authority figures or mentors could play a helpful role now, offering guidance that shapes your next steps. Avoid scattering your energy across too many directions; focus instead on the path that feels most meaningful. Strategic, authentic action will bring lasting results.

Affirmation & Gratitude

"I am grateful for clarity in my ambitions and the courage to follow them."

Gemini
05-September-2026

The cosmos invites you inward, Gemini, reminding you of the importance of stillness and reflection. Today is not about pushing forward but about restoring balance. Pay attention to dreams, inner nudges, or intuitive insights—they may reveal truths you've been overlooking. Avoid overloading yourself with obligations and allow yourself time to rest. Creative practices, meditation, or journaling will feel especially rewarding now. By slowing down, you open space for clarity and renewal. Trust that pausing is part of your progress, not a delay.

Affirmation & Gratitude
"I honour rest and reflection, trusting they restore my clarity and strength."

Gemini

06-September-2026

Fresh energy fills your day, Gemini, bringing confidence, courage, and self-expression. This is a great time to start a project, take initiative, or embrace a new opportunity. People are drawn to your enthusiasm, and your lively energy may inspire others as well. Avoid scattering your focus—choose one direction that excites you most and commit to it fully. The universe supports bold, authentic moves today, so trust your instincts. Step into your individuality with pride—it's your greatest strength. Your originality shines brightest when you share it openly.

Affirmation & Gratitude

"I celebrate my individuality and step into new beginnings with confidence."

Gemini

07-September-2026

Relationships are highlighted again, Gemini, and the stars remind you of the importance of balance and cooperation. Conversations today may hold extra weight, offering opportunities to resolve misunderstandings or deepen trust. Don't gloss over issues—your gift for words allows you to approach them gently yet honestly. If single, this is a favourable day for meeting someone aligned with your energy. If partnered, this is a chance to strengthen your bond through authenticity and patience. Relationships grow stronger when nurtured with both honesty and kindness.

Affirmation & Gratitude

"I am grateful for the trust and love that enrich my relationships."

Gemini

03-September-2026

Gemini, practical matters step into focus today. This is a day to handle responsibilities tied to health, work, or organisation. While these tasks may not feel exciting, they're essential for long-term stability. Avoid multitasking—choose one important job and give it your full attention. You'll feel lighter and more accomplished afterward. Think of today as planting seeds of discipline that will grow into freedom later. By tending to these details, you build a strong foundation for your bigger dreams and adventures. Balance comes from embracing both responsibility and spontaneity.

Affirmation & Gratitude

"I am thankful for routines that bring balance, stability, and peace of mind."

Gemini
09-September-2026

Adventure energy rises once more, Gemini, urging you to expand your horizons. This could involve travel, study, or simply engaging with fresh ideas and people who challenge your perspective. Your mind thrives on variety, and today offers plenty of opportunities to feed it. Don't shy away from experiences just because they're unfamiliar—these are the ones that spark the most growth. Follow your curiosity boldly, and you may uncover a new passion or path that excites your spirit. Inspiration is waiting for you just beyond your comfort zone.

Affirmation & Gratitude

"I welcome new experiences that expand my mind and spirit with joy."

Gemini
10-September-2026

Gemini, career matters and ambitions come to the forefront today. Recognition for your work may arrive, or you may feel motivated to define your goals more clearly. The stars remind you that true success lies in aligning your professional path with your authentic self. Authority figures or mentors may offer valuable advice now—listen closely. Avoid spreading your energy too thin; choose one meaningful direction and commit. By stepping into your confidence and clarity, you'll build momentum that lasts well into the future. This is a day for purposeful action.

Affirmation & Gratitude

"I am grateful for clarity in my goals and the courage to pursue them."

Gemini
11-September-2026

The cosmos draws you inward today, encouraging reflection and rest. Gemini, while your airy nature thrives on activity, balance requires stillness too. Pay attention to dreams, gut feelings, or subtle nudges—they may reveal the answers you've been seeking. Don't overload your day; instead, prioritise quiet time, journaling, or meditation. This pause is not wasted time—it's where clarity and inspiration are born. Trust that by honouring your inner world, you are preparing yourself for fresh momentum and opportunities soon to come.

Affirmation & Gratitude

"I honour rest and reflection as powerful tools for clarity and renewal."

Gemini
12-September-2026

A burst of vibrant energy surrounds you, Gemini, filling you with confidence, motivation, and creativity. This is a perfect day to take initiative, launch a project, or showcase your talents. Others are drawn to your charm and originality, so opportunities may arise unexpectedly. Avoid scattering your energy—channel your enthusiasm into one meaningful pursuit. The universe supports bold, authentic moves today, reminding you that your individuality is your greatest strength. Step into the spotlight without hesitation—you're ready to shine.

Affirmation & Gratitude

"I celebrate my uniqueness and take bold steps toward my dreams with joy."

Gemini
13-September-2026

Gemini, relationships are in the spotlight again, highlighting balance, compromise, and connection. Use your natural communication skills to strengthen bonds and address any lingering issues. Honest conversations may bring breakthroughs, deepening trust with those closest to you. If single, this is a favourable day to meet someone through social circles or shared interests. If partnered, today supports collaboration and renewed understanding. Harmony doesn't come from avoiding conflict but from addressing it with respect. Authenticity will strengthen the bonds you value most.

Affirmation & Gratitude

"I am thankful for relationships that grow stronger through honesty and mutual respect."

Gemini
14-September-2026

Practical matters come into focus, Gemini. This is a day to get organised, prioritise health, and handle responsibilities with care. While routine may feel restrictive, the stars remind you that structure provides freedom. Focus on one or two important tasks and complete them fully. Productivity flows when you simplify and ground yourself. These small but consistent efforts will strengthen your foundation, leaving you more space for creativity and exploration later. By honouring discipline today, you set yourself up for balance tomorrow.

Affirmation & Gratitude

"I am grateful for the routines and habits that keep my life balanced and stable."

Gemini
15-September-2026

Adventure beckons once again, Gemini, stirring your restlessness and curiosity. The universe invites you to seek new knowledge, travel, or experiences that push you outside your comfort zone. Conversations with people who think differently may spark inspiration and fresh ideas. Don't let fear of the unknown hold you back—your adaptability makes you ready for change. Today is about trusting your curiosity as a guide. Growth and excitement are waiting if you're willing to step into unfamiliar territory with courage and openness.

Affirmation & Gratitude

"I welcome new perspectives and embrace the growth they bring into my journey."

Gemini

16-September-2026

Gemini, your career and ambitions step back into the spotlight today. You may feel recognition for past efforts or a push to refine your goals. The stars are asking you to align your professional path with your authentic values. Authority figures or mentors could provide feedback that helps shape your direction—listen closely, but trust your instincts too. Avoid scattering your attention across too many opportunities; clarity comes when you choose one meaningful direction and follow through. Today is about progress rooted in both vision and strategy.

Affirmation & Gratitude

"I am grateful for clarity in my ambitions and the courage to pursue them authentically."

Gemini
17-September-2026

The cosmos turns your focus inward, encouraging you to pause and reflect. Gemini, while you thrive on variety and movement, stillness is equally important. This is a good day to recharge through quiet activities such as journaling, meditation, or creative expression. Pay attention to your dreams and intuition—they may reveal guidance you've overlooked. Don't push yourself into overactivity; slowing down will help you process emotions and regain clarity. Trust that rest is not wasted time but a vital part of your growth. Honour your inner world with patience today.

Affirmation & Gratitude

"I honour stillness and trust the wisdom it brings into my life."

Gemini
18-September-2026

Fresh energy surrounds you, Gemini, sparking confidence and creativity. This is an excellent day for bold action, self-expression, or beginning something new. Your wit and charm make you magnetic, and people may be drawn to your ideas. The universe supports authenticity now, so don't dim your individuality to please others. Focus your enthusiasm on one inspired project rather than scattering it in many directions. When you lead with confidence and truth, opportunities unfold naturally. The stars encourage you to act decisively and trust in your originality.

Affirmation & Gratitude

"I celebrate my individuality and embrace new beginnings with courage and joy."

Gemini
19-September-2026

Relationships take focus today, Gemini. Balance, honesty, and patience will strengthen your bonds. If issues have been lingering, this is a good day to resolve them through open and respectful conversation. Your ability to lighten heavy topics with humour can help, but remember that depth is required for true harmony. If single, you may feel drawn to someone intriguing, while those partnered may rediscover connection through shared goals. Relationships flourish when both sides feel heard, valued, and respected. Show up authentically, and harmony will follow.

Affirmation & Gratitude

"I am grateful for the trust and respect that nurture my relationships."

Gemini

20-September-2026

Gemini, practical responsibilities rise to the surface today. Focus on work, health, or organisation, and avoid scattering your energy in too many directions. Small steps—like tidying your space, revising your budget, or committing to self-care—will provide a sense of accomplishment and balance. The stars remind you that structure doesn't limit your freedom; it creates it. Productivity flows when you focus on one task at a time. These efforts may feel small now, but they create a lasting foundation for the dreams you're building.

Affirmation & Gratitude

"I am thankful for the routines and structure that support my freedom and growth."

Gemini

21-September-2026

Adventure energy rises again, Gemini, inspiring you to seek out new knowledge, perspectives, and experiences. Whether through travel, study, or thought-provoking conversations, today is about expansion. Don't shy away from ideas that challenge your current beliefs—growth often lies in discomfort. Follow your curiosity boldly, and you may uncover inspiration that reshapes your path. The universe is reminding you that your adaptability is your greatest strength. Use it to navigate new territory with excitement, not fear. Opportunities for learning and expansion are abundant now.

Affirmation & Gratitude

"I welcome new perspectives and the growth they bring into my journey."

Gemini

22-September-2026

Gemini, your career and long-term ambitions are highlighted once again. Recognition for your talents may arrive, or you may feel motivated to push forward with your goals. Use this energy for strategic planning and authentic action. Align your ambitions with your deeper values to ensure lasting fulfilment. Guidance from a mentor or colleague may help clarify your path—be open to advice but stay true to yourself. This is a powerful day to step into the spotlight confidently and showcase your adaptability and charm.

Affirmation & Gratitude

"I am grateful for clarity in my goals and the courage to pursue them with authenticity."

Gemini
23-September-2026

Gemini, today the cosmos encourages you to turn inward and reflect. After a busy period of outward focus, your inner world needs attention. Don't push yourself into constant activity—make space for rest, journaling, or meditation. Your intuition is strong now, and subtle insights could provide answers you've been seeking. Allow yourself to unplug from outside noise so your spirit can recharge. Trust that even when you pause, growth is unfolding behind the scenes. Balance is created when you honour both your inner and outer worlds equally.

Affirmation & Gratitude

"I honour rest and trust my intuition to guide me with wisdom and clarity."

Gemini
24-September-2026

Fresh energy flows through your day, Gemini, inspiring confidence, creativity, and bold action. This is a great time to showcase your talents, start something new, or pursue a goal with determination. Your charisma makes you magnetic, drawing opportunities and people your way. Focus your energy carefully—don't scatter it across too many directions. By committing to one meaningful project, you'll see real progress. The universe supports authenticity today, so lead with your individuality and let your unique perspective shine. Others will be inspired by your courage.

Affirmation & Gratitude
"I celebrate my individuality and step forward with courage and joy."

Gemini
25-September-2026

Relationships and partnerships are highlighted today. Gemini, you may find yourself navigating balance, compromise, and cooperation. If tensions arise, use your natural communication skills to resolve them with patience and clarity. Avoid glossing over important matters with humour—authenticity is needed for harmony to thrive. If single, you may connect with someone who sparks your curiosity. If partnered, today offers the chance to deepen trust and reaffirm shared goals. Remember, meaningful connections grow stronger when both sides feel heard and respected equally.

Affirmation & Gratitude
"I am grateful for the love and balance that strengthen my connections."

Gemini
26-September-2026

Gemini, practical responsibilities call your attention today. This is a time to focus on organisation, health, and routines. While your airy energy prefers spontaneity, the stars remind you that discipline provides the freedom you love. Take on one or two important tasks instead of overwhelming yourself. Even small steps—like decluttering, meal planning, or financial organisation—can create lasting stability. Productivity flows when you avoid multitasking and work steadily. Think of today as fine-tuning the foundations that support your bigger goals. Balance is found through structure and flexibility.

Affirmation & Gratitude
"I am thankful for the steady habits that keep my life balanced and secure."

Gemini
27-September-2026

Adventure energy stirs again, Gemini, urging you to explore beyond your usual boundaries. This is an excellent day for learning, travel, or seeking inspiration through new ideas and perspectives. Conversations with people who see the world differently could spark revelations. Don't hold back from trying something unfamiliar—it may lead to growth in unexpected ways. Your natural adaptability makes you ready for change, so step boldly into the unknown. Inspiration and renewal await if you follow your curiosity with courage and openness today.

Affirmation & Gratitude

"I welcome new experiences and embrace the wisdom they bring into my journey."

Gemini
28-September-2026

Career and ambitions come to the forefront today, Gemini. Recognition for your work is possible, or you may feel a renewed drive to refine your long-term goals. This is a day to think strategically: align your efforts with your true values for lasting fulfilment. Mentors or colleagues may offer guidance, so stay open to their insights. Avoid spreading yourself too thin; focus instead on what feels most authentic and sustainable. Success flows naturally when you combine clarity, adaptability, and authenticity. The universe supports your growth.

Affirmation & Gratitude

"I am grateful for clarity in my ambitions and the courage to pursue them."

Gemini
29-September-2026

Gemini, the cosmos calls you inward again. After days of outward focus, your inner world craves stillness and renewal. This is a time to rest, reflect, and listen to your intuition. Subtle signs, dreams, or creative impulses may reveal insights about your next steps. Don't overload yourself with obligations—prioritise peace and self-care. Reflection restores clarity and balance, preparing you for the fresh energy soon to come. Trust that this pause is just as valuable as forward momentum; it nurtures your mind, body, and spirit.

Affirmation & Gratitude

"I honour reflection and trust the stillness to restore my clarity and strength."

Gemini
30-September-2026

Fresh energy fills the air today, Gemini, lifting your confidence and inspiring bold action. This is the perfect day to step into the spotlight, showcase your talents, or start something new. Your natural charm and quick wit make you magnetic, attracting support and opportunities. Focus is key, though—avoid scattering your energy across too many ideas. Choose one inspired path and pursue it with enthusiasm. The stars encourage you to act courageously and authentically. Trust that by leading with your individuality, you'll open doors that bring long-term growth and fulfilment.

Affirmation & Gratitude

"I celebrate my individuality and take bold, confident steps toward my dreams."

October 2026

Gemini
01-October-2026

Relationships and partnerships are highlighted today, Gemini. Whether romantic, friendly, or professional, the stars remind you that balance and open communication are key. You may need to compromise or address unresolved issues. Use your gift for words to bridge gaps, but remember that listening is just as important as speaking. If single, you could meet someone intriguing. If partnered, today is about deepening trust and reaffirming shared goals. True harmony is built on honesty and respect, not surface-level agreements. Show up authentically, and your connections will flourish.

Affirmation & Gratitude

"I am grateful for relationships strengthened by honesty, trust, and respect."

Gemini
02-October-2026

Gemini, practical matters come into focus today. While your adaptable nature prefers variety, the stars encourage you to ground yourself in responsibilities. Focus on health, finances, or organisation. Small, steady steps now will create long-term stability. Don't overwhelm yourself with too much at once—prioritise one or two tasks and complete them fully. Productivity feels satisfying today, and you'll gain peace of mind knowing you're building a stronger foundation for the future. Structure doesn't restrict you; it frees you to explore with confidence. Balance is found through both routine and adventure.

Affirmation & Gratitude

"I am thankful for the routines that bring balance, health, and stability."

Gemini
03-October-2026

Adventure calls again, Gemini, and your curiosity is buzzing. This is an excellent day for exploring new places, learning something fresh, or connecting with people who broaden your perspective. Don't shy away from experiences that challenge your comfort zone—they're the ones that will spark the greatest growth. Your mind is hungry for inspiration, and the universe is providing plenty today. Whether through travel, study, or conversation, seek out opportunities that expand your worldview and renew your spirit. Trust your curiosity; it's your greatest guide.

Affirmation & Gratitude

"I welcome new perspectives and embrace the wisdom they bring to my life."

Gemini
04-October-2026

Career and ambitions step into focus today, Gemini. Recognition for your skills may arrive, or you may feel a renewed drive to pursue long-term goals. The stars encourage you to align your ambitions with your deeper values. Authority figures or mentors could provide insights that guide your next steps—listen with openness, but trust your instincts too. Don't scatter your energy across too many paths; clarity comes from focusing on what feels truly meaningful. Strategic, authentic action today will create momentum that carries into the weeks ahead.

Affirmation & Gratitude

"I am grateful for clarity in my goals and the courage to act on them."

Gemini
05-October-2026

The cosmos calls you inward, Gemini, inviting you to slow down and reflect. After days of activity, your spirit needs time to recharge. Pay attention to your inner world—intuition, dreams, or quiet nudges may bring valuable guidance. Avoid overloading your schedule; instead, create space for rest, meditation, or creative expression. Trust that by stepping back, you're allowing clarity to surface. Balance isn't only about movement and growth—it's also about honouring your need for stillness. This pause is part of your progress, not separate from it.

Affirmation & Gratitude

"I honour rest and trust my inner wisdom to guide me forward."

Gemini
06-October-2026

Fresh, lively energy returns today, Gemini, filling you with confidence and momentum. This is the time to take initiative, launch projects, or step forward with bold ideas. People are drawn to your magnetic presence, and opportunities may arise simply because of your authentic energy. Avoid diluting your efforts across too many ventures—focus instead on one inspired path. The stars encourage authenticity above all else. By trusting yourself and embracing your individuality, you'll not only create progress but also inspire those around you.

Affirmation & Gratitude

"I celebrate my uniqueness and embrace the courage to shine authentically."

Gemini
07-October-2026

Gemini, relationships are emphasised today, asking you to focus on cooperation, balance, and open-hearted communication. Whether in romance, friendship, or business, the stars encourage you to engage in honest conversations. Avoid brushing aside important topics with humour—authenticity is what strengthens trust. If single, this is a favourable day to meet someone intriguing who resonates with your energy. If partnered, it's a good time to reaffirm shared goals and deepen your bond. Relationships thrive when both sides feel seen, heard, and respected equally. Authenticity is your key to harmony now.

Affirmation & Gratitude

"I am grateful for relationships built on honesty, balance, and mutual respect."

Gemini
08-October-2026

Today highlights routines, health, and responsibilities, Gemini. While your airy nature thrives on variety, the cosmos reminds you of the stability structure provides. This is a great day to organise your space, revisit your budget, or refine your schedule. Avoid multitasking; instead, commit fully to one task and complete it. Small, consistent efforts will create long-term balance and free your energy for more spontaneous pursuits. Remember, discipline is not your enemy—it's the key to building the flexibility you crave. By tending to details today, you support your bigger dreams tomorrow.

Affirmation & Gratitude

"I am thankful for the steady habits that bring balance and stability."

Gemini
09-October-2026

Adventure calls once again, Gemini, and your curiosity is lit up. This is a perfect day for exploring new knowledge, trying something unfamiliar, or seeking experiences that push you outside your comfort zone. Travel, study, or inspiring conversations may spark ideas that reshape your outlook. Don't be afraid to step boldly into the unknown—the universe is encouraging you to trust your adaptability. Growth happens when you allow curiosity to lead. Today, you'll discover inspiration that fuels your future path in exciting and unexpected ways.

Affirmation & Gratitude
"I welcome new experiences that expand my perspective and inspire my journey."

Gemini
10-October-2026

Gemini, career and ambitions step into focus today. Recognition may come from authority figures, or you may feel the drive to refine your long-term goals. This is not the time to scatter your energy—clarity and focus will bring better results. Align your professional path with your deeper values, ensuring your definition of success feels authentic. Seek guidance from trusted mentors if needed, but remember to trust your instincts too. The stars encourage you to step forward confidently, knowing that steady, strategic effort will lead you to meaningful progress.

Affirmation & Gratitude

"I am grateful for clarity in my career and the courage to pursue my goals."

Gemini
11-October-2026

The cosmos turns your focus inward today, Gemini. Your spirit craves stillness and reflection after days of outward action. Pay attention to intuition, dreams, or subtle signs—they may provide answers you've been overlooking. Don't overload your schedule; instead, carve out space for quiet reflection, journaling, or meditation. Balance comes from honouring both your need for activity and your need for rest. Trust that pausing is part of progress, not a step backward. By creating stillness today, you prepare yourself for fresh clarity and renewed energy tomorrow.

Affirmation & Gratitude

"I honour rest and trust the wisdom that arises in stillness."

Gemini

12-October-2026

Fresh energy flows through your day, Gemini, inspiring confidence, motivation, and creativity. This is a day for bold self-expression, starting new ventures, or showcasing your talents. Others are drawn to your charm and originality, and opportunities may present themselves as a result. Avoid scattering your energy in too many directions; focus on what excites you most. The universe is encouraging authenticity—be yourself fully, and you'll see progress unfold naturally. Your individuality is your greatest gift, and today is the perfect day to share it openly.

Affirmation & Gratitude

"I celebrate my uniqueness and embrace opportunities with courage and joy."

Gemini
13-October-2026

Relationships and partnerships are highlighted again today. Gemini, you may need to compromise or engage in heartfelt conversations that bring clarity and balance. Use your gift for communication to build bridges, but don't avoid deeper truths. If single, new encounters could feel promising and spark excitement. If partnered, this is a chance to strengthen your bond by reaffirming your commitment. True harmony isn't about avoiding differences—it's about working through them with patience and honesty. The stars remind you that authentic connection is always worth the effort.

Affirmation & Gratitude

"I am thankful for the love and respect that nurture my relationships."

Gemini
14-October-2026

Gemini, today's energy highlights routines, health, and responsibilities. While your adaptable spirit prefers variety, the stars remind you that structure creates the freedom you crave. This is an excellent day to focus on practical matters—organising your schedule, addressing finances, or paying attention to your wellbeing. Productivity will flow if you commit to one task at a time instead of juggling too much. Even small, steady steps now create long-term stability. Think of today as strengthening the foundation that supports your bigger goals and adventures. Balance between discipline and exploration is essential.

Affirmation & Gratitude

"I am grateful for routines that support my health, balance, and freedom."

Gemini
15-October-2026

Adventure calls once again, Gemini, filling you with curiosity and restlessness. The cosmos encourages you to expand your horizons, whether through travel, learning, or conversations that broaden your perspective. Don't shy away from new experiences simply because they feel unfamiliar—these are the ones that spark growth. Today, inspiration may come from unexpected sources, and your natural adaptability makes you ready to embrace it. Follow your curiosity with courage, and you'll discover opportunities that energise your spirit and shape your future path. Growth often begins where comfort ends.

Affirmation & Gratitude

"I welcome new experiences and the wisdom they bring into my journey."

Gemini
16-October-2026

Gemini, career and ambitions step into focus again. Recognition may come for your past efforts, or you may feel motivated to set clearer goals. This is a day for aligning your long-term vision with your daily actions. Authority figures or mentors could provide helpful guidance, so be open to input. Avoid scattering your energy across too many pursuits; clarity will come from focusing on what feels most authentic to you. By taking purposeful steps now, you create momentum that carries you closer to your aspirations.

Affirmation & Gratitude

"I am grateful for clarity in my goals and the courage to act authentically."

Gemini
17-October-2026

The cosmos encourages reflection and rest today. Gemini, your airy nature loves movement, but your soul needs stillness to restore balance. Intuition is heightened—listen to your inner voice for guidance. Avoid overloading your schedule; instead, carve out time for solitude, meditation, or creative outlets that soothe you. Insights may come through dreams or subtle nudges, so pay attention. Trust that by pausing, you're creating space for clarity and renewal. Balance is achieved not by constant motion but by honouring both action and stillness equally.

Affirmation & Gratitude

"I honour stillness and trust my inner wisdom to guide me forward."

Gemini
18-October-2026

A fresh burst of energy surrounds you today, Gemini, boosting your confidence and vitality. This is the perfect day for bold self-expression, new beginnings, or stepping into the spotlight. Others are drawn to your charm and enthusiasm, so opportunities may arise unexpectedly. The stars encourage you to focus your energy rather than scatter it—choose one direction that excites you most and commit fully. Authenticity is your superpower, and when you lead with it, progress flows naturally. Celebrate your individuality today—it's what sets you apart.

Affirmation & Gratitude

"I celebrate my individuality and embrace opportunities with courage and joy."

Gemini
19-October-2026

Relationships and partnerships take centre stage again today. Gemini, whether in love, friendship, or business, balance and cooperation are key. Use your gift for communication to foster harmony, but remember that listening is just as important as speaking. If single, you may encounter someone who intrigues you. If partnered, this is a chance to strengthen your bond through openness and mutual understanding. Don't shy away from difficult conversations—they build deeper trust. Authenticity and patience will ensure your connections thrive in the long run.

Affirmation & Gratitude

"I am grateful for relationships built on honesty, respect, and trust."

Gemini
20-October-2026

Gemini, today is about grounding yourself in responsibilities and routines. The stars highlight health, organisation, and the small details that create balance. While you love spontaneity, tending to practical matters now will support your future freedom. Productivity will flow if you focus on one priority at a time instead of scattering your attention. Even small steps—like tidying your space, creating a plan, or making time for self-care—will ripple into lasting stability. Think of today as investing in your long-term wellbeing and success.

Affirmation & Gratitude

"I am thankful for the habits and routines that support balance and stability."

Gemini
21-October-2026

Adventure energy rises today, Gemini, urging you to step outside of your comfort zone. This could involve travel, study, or conversations with people who challenge your thinking. Your mind craves stimulation, and the cosmos is providing plenty of opportunities for growth. Don't dismiss new experiences simply because they feel uncertain—these are the ones that spark expansion. Inspiration may arrive in unexpected places, opening the door to ideas that shape your future. Say yes to exploration, and you'll discover the excitement and wisdom that comes from embracing the unknown.

Affirmation & Gratitude

"I welcome new experiences and the wisdom they bring into my journey."

Gemini

22-October-2026

Gemini, career and ambition take the spotlight today. Recognition may come your way, or you may feel the drive to clarify your long-term vision. This is a good day to align your goals with your authentic self. Success feels most rewarding when it reflects your values as well as your talents. Conversations with mentors or authority figures could help guide your next steps—remain open but trust your instincts. The universe encourages you to step forward with confidence, using your adaptability as a strength.

Affirmation & Gratitude

"I am grateful for clarity in my ambitions and the courage to pursue them."

Gemini
23-October-2026

The cosmos encourages reflection today, Gemini. After days of forward focus, your soul craves balance and stillness. Take time to slow down, journal, meditate, or simply be with your thoughts. Intuition is heightened, and subtle insights may bring clarity about a decision or your next steps. Avoid overloading your schedule—rest and stillness will serve you best. Trust that pausing doesn't halt progress; it prepares you for the energy and opportunities ahead. Honour this inward turn—it restores strength and wisdom for what's next.

Affirmation & Gratitude
"I honour stillness and trust my inner wisdom to guide me forward."

Gemini

24-October-2026

A fresh surge of energy surrounds you today, Gemini. Confidence, creativity, and motivation are strong, making this a great time to start a project or showcase your talents. People are drawn to your lively spirit, and opportunities may arise simply because of your openness and charm. Avoid scattering your focus—choose one pursuit that excites you and commit to it fully. The stars encourage bold self-expression and authenticity now. When you lead with your individuality, progress flows naturally, and doors open. Step into your courage and shine.

Affirmation & Gratitude

"I celebrate my uniqueness and embrace bold new opportunities with joy."

Gemini
25-October-2026

Relationships are highlighted, Gemini. The cosmos encourages balance, compromise, and heartfelt communication. If there's been tension, today is a good time to clear the air and strengthen trust. Use your humour and honesty to navigate conversations, but don't avoid important truths—depth is necessary for growth. If single, you may find a connection through shared interests or social settings. If partnered, this is a beautiful day to reaffirm your commitment and strengthen bonds. Harmony comes from showing up authentically and being open to listening as well as speaking.

Affirmation & Gratitude

"I am grateful for the love and trust that nurture my relationships."

Gemini
26-October-2026

Gemini, today brings a focus on routines, health, and organisation. The cosmos reminds you that structure supports the freedom you love. Take small steps toward order—tidy your environment, revisit your schedule, or commit to healthier habits. Don't overwhelm yourself with too much; instead, focus on one priority and complete it fully. These steady efforts create stability and peace of mind. Think of today as building the foundation that supports your energy for bigger dreams. Balance is achieved when discipline and spontaneity work together in harmony.

Affirmation & Gratitude

"I am thankful for routines that create balance and stability in my life."

Gemini
27-October-2026

Adventure energy returns, filling you with curiosity and restlessness. This is the perfect time to explore new places, ideas, or conversations that broaden your perspective. Don't hold back from trying something unfamiliar—your adaptability makes you ready for change. Growth often begins when you say yes to the unknown. Feed your spirit with fresh experiences, and you may discover new passions or opportunities that inspire you. The universe is reminding you that curiosity is your compass—trust it, and it will guide you toward expansion.

Affirmation & Gratitude

"I welcome adventure and the growth it brings to my mind and spirit."

Gemini
28-October-2026

Gemini, today the spotlight shines on your career and ambitions. Recognition may arrive, or you may feel a renewed push to define your long-term goals more clearly. This is a good time to align your ambitions with your authentic values, ensuring that the success you pursue feels meaningful. A mentor, colleague, or authority figure may provide guidance, but remember to trust your instincts above all. Avoid scattering your energy—focus on one significant step forward. Progress now is about blending strategy with authenticity, creating momentum that lasts.

Affirmation & Gratitude

"I am grateful for clarity in my goals and the courage to follow them."

Gemini

29-October-2026

The cosmos encourages reflection and inner focus today, Gemini. After recent outward action, your soul craves stillness and renewal. Don't overload your schedule—create space for peace, meditation, or journaling. Your intuition is heightened, and dreams or quiet nudges may reveal truths you've been overlooking. This is not a day to push or force results; clarity will surface naturally when you allow yourself to pause. Remember, growth is not only about doing—it's also about being. Honour your inner world, and you'll return with renewed perspective and strength.

Affirmation & Gratitude

"I honour stillness and trust my inner wisdom to guide me with clarity."

Gemini
30-October-2026

Fresh, vibrant energy fills your day, Gemini, bringing confidence and boldness. This is an ideal time to embrace self-expression, start something new, or share your talents more widely. People are drawn to your natural charm and adaptability, and opportunities may come through unexpected avenues. The stars encourage you to act authentically, committing to one inspired path rather than scattering your energy across too many. When you lead with courage and individuality, you'll find yourself creating momentum that inspires not only you but those around you.

Affirmation & Gratitude

"I celebrate my uniqueness and take confident steps toward my dreams."

Gemini

31-October-2026

Relationships come into focus today, Gemini, and the stars ask you to seek harmony and balance. Whether in romance, friendship, or business, meaningful conversations may help resolve misunderstandings or deepen trust. Use your wit and warmth to navigate sensitive topics, but avoid avoiding deeper truths—authenticity matters most. If you're single, this is a favourable time to meet someone intriguing. If partnered, this is a beautiful day to reaffirm commitment and appreciation. By showing up honestly and compassionately, your connections will grow stronger and more resilient.

Affirmation & Gratitude

"I am thankful for the love and trust that enrich my relationships."

November 2026

Gemini

01-November-2026

Gemini, the cosmos highlights routines, health, and responsibilities today. While you love spontaneity, the stars remind you that discipline creates balance. Focus on tasks you may have been putting off—organising your space, reviewing your budget, or tending to your physical wellbeing. Avoid multitasking and give your energy to one thing at a time. Small, consistent steps create stability and free you for future adventures. Today is about building habits that support your growth in the long run. Structure and freedom are not opposites—they complement one another beautifully.

Affirmation & Gratitude

"I am grateful for routines that bring balance, health, and stability into my life."

Gemini

02-November-2026

Adventure energy stirs once again, Gemini, filling you with restlessness and curiosity. This is a wonderful day to seek out inspiration through travel, study, or conversations with people who challenge your thinking. Don't shy away from the unfamiliar—it may provide the breakthrough you've been waiting for. Your natural adaptability makes you well-equipped to explore new territory. By saying yes to opportunities today, you invite excitement and growth. The universe reminds you that curiosity is your compass—follow it, and it will guide you toward expansion.

Affirmation & Gratitude

"I welcome new perspectives and embrace the wisdom they bring."

Gemini
03-November-2026

Career and ambitions are highlighted today, Gemini. Recognition may arrive, or you may feel compelled to take action toward your long-term vision. The stars encourage strategy and focus—avoid scattering your energy across too many opportunities. Seek guidance from mentors or authority figures who can provide valuable perspective, but always stay true to your authentic self. When you align your actions with your values, success flows naturally. This is a day for confident, purposeful steps that move you closer to the goals you've set for yourself.

Affirmation & Gratitude

"I am grateful for clarity in my ambitions and the courage to act authentically."

Gemini
04-November-2026

Gemini, the cosmos turns your attention inward today. After recent momentum, your spirit craves reflection and rest. This is not the time to push ahead but to allow stillness to guide you. Pay attention to dreams, intuitive nudges, or synchronicities—they may reveal answers you've been seeking. Give yourself space from distractions, and clarity will naturally surface. Gentle self-care and creative expression will be especially nourishing. Trust that slowing down isn't wasted time—it's part of your journey. By honouring your need for rest, you prepare yourself for the fresh energy soon to come.

Affirmation & Gratitude

"I honour rest and reflection, trusting they restore my clarity and strength."

Gemini
05-November-2026

Fresh energy fills the day, Gemini, sparking motivation, creativity, and boldness. This is a great time to showcase your talents, take initiative, or begin a new project. People are drawn to your light-hearted charm and originality, so opportunities may appear unexpectedly. Avoid scattering your efforts—focus on one direction where you can truly shine. The universe encourages you to step forward with courage and authenticity. By embracing your individuality today, you'll create momentum that inspires not only you but also those around you. Trust your spark—it will guide you well.

Affirmation & Gratitude

"I celebrate my uniqueness and embrace new opportunities with courage."

Gemini
06-November-2026

Relationships and partnerships are highlighted today, Gemini. Whether in romance, friendship, or professional connections, the cosmos asks you to focus on cooperation, balance, and honest communication. Use your gift for words to strengthen bonds, but remember that listening is just as important as speaking. If single, a new connection may spark through shared interests or social settings. If partnered, today is a chance to reaffirm trust and mutual respect. Authentic exchanges will bring harmony and deepen connections. Show up fully and honestly—you'll find your relationships flourishing with renewed strength.

Affirmation & Gratitude

"I am grateful for the love, balance, and trust in my relationships."

Gemini
07-November-2026

Gemini, today the stars highlight health, organisation, and responsibilities. While your airy spirit thrives on variety, the cosmos reminds you of the grounding power of structure. Focus on small, manageable tasks that bring order to your life—whether tidying your environment, revisiting your schedule, or tending to your physical wellbeing. Avoid multitasking; productivity will flow when you simplify and give your attention to one priority at a time. By honouring the details today, you create the freedom to explore tomorrow. Think of this as strengthening the base that supports your adventurous soul.

Affirmation & Gratitude

"I am thankful for the routines that bring balance and stability into my life."

Gemini
08-November-2026

Adventure calls again, Gemini, and the universe encourages you to step outside your comfort zone. Curiosity is your greatest guide today—follow it into new experiences, study, or travel. Conversations with people who hold different perspectives may shift your thinking in powerful ways. Don't shy away from unfamiliar paths; they may lead to growth you didn't expect. Your adaptability makes you well-suited to embrace change with excitement rather than fear. Trust the process of exploration—it will awaken your spirit and inspire your future steps. Say yes to discovery.

Affirmation & Gratitude

"I welcome new perspectives and the wisdom they bring into my journey."

Gemini
09-November-2026

Gemini, career and ambitions come into sharp focus today. Recognition for past efforts may arrive, or you may feel called to refine your long-term goals with greater clarity. Authority figures or mentors could play a supportive role, offering valuable guidance. Don't spread your energy too thin—focus on what feels most authentic and meaningful. Success flows best when it aligns with your deeper values. This is a day to combine strategy with courage, trusting your unique vision. Stand confidently in your individuality—your path is unfolding exactly as it should.

Affirmation & Gratitude

"I am grateful for clarity in my goals and the courage to act authentically."

Gemini
10-November-2026

The cosmos calls you inward today, Gemini, reminding you of the power of rest and reflection. After recent external focus, your inner world needs attention. Give yourself space to slow down and listen to your intuition. Subtle insights may reveal truths you've been overlooking. Don't pressure yourself to keep moving forward—sometimes the greatest progress is made in stillness. Journaling, meditation, or creative expression will feel especially restorative. Trust that by honouring rest, you're creating space for clarity and inspiration to rise. Balance requires both action and stillness.

Affirmation & Gratitude

"I honour rest as a vital part of my growth and clarity."

Gemini
11-November-2026

Gemini, fresh energy surrounds you today, bringing confidence, courage, and creativity. This is an ideal time to take initiative, launch a project, or showcase your talents. People are drawn to your magnetic presence, and opportunities may arise simply because of your authenticity. Avoid scattering your efforts across too many directions; focus instead on one inspired path. When you act boldly and embrace your individuality, you'll create lasting momentum. The stars remind you that progress comes when you trust yourself enough to shine unapologetically.

Affirmation & Gratitude

"I celebrate my individuality and embrace new beginnings with courage and joy."

Gemini
12-November-2026

Relationships are highlighted, Gemini, and the cosmos encourages balance, compromise, and honest exchanges. This is a powerful day to address lingering issues or to deepen bonds through meaningful conversations. If single, you may encounter someone intriguing who sparks your curiosity. If partnered, today offers opportunities to reaffirm your commitment and rediscover connection. Remember, harmony doesn't come from avoiding differences—it comes from respecting and working through them. Your ability to blend humour with honesty makes you a natural at keeping communication flowing with ease and warmth.

Affirmation & Gratitude

"I am grateful for the trust, love, and honesty that strengthen my relationships."

Gemini
13-November-2026

Gemini, practical matters come to the forefront today. While your restless spirit prefers variety, the stars are asking you to ground yourself in structure and detail. Focus on health, finances, or organisation, and avoid multitasking. Productivity flows when you take one step at a time. These small but consistent actions create the stability that allows you to embrace spontaneity later. Think of today as setting the stage for your bigger goals—strengthening your foundation so you can leap higher tomorrow. Balance between responsibility and freedom is essential.

Affirmation & Gratitude

"I am thankful for the routines and habits that bring balance and stability."

Gemini
14-November-2026

Adventure energy rises again, Gemini, filling you with curiosity and excitement. This is a great day to step outside your comfort zone, whether through travel, study, or exploring fresh ideas. Conversations with people who challenge your perspective may spark new inspiration. Don't be afraid to experiment with something unfamiliar—the unknown often holds the greatest rewards. The universe encourages you to follow your curiosity boldly. Your adaptability will help you thrive no matter what comes your way. Inspiration awaits in the spaces you've yet to explore.

Affirmation & Gratitude

"I welcome new experiences and the wisdom they bring to my journey."

Gemini
15-November-2026

Gemini, career and ambitions are emphasised today. Recognition for your work may arrive, or you may feel motivated to refine your long-term goals. Use this energy strategically, aligning your efforts with your authentic values. Mentors or authority figures could provide useful guidance, so be open to feedback. Don't scatter your energy across too many opportunities—choose the direction that feels most fulfilling and sustainable. This is a day to step forward confidently, knowing that progress comes from aligning vision with authenticity. The stars support you in building momentum now.

Affirmation & Gratitude

"I am grateful for clarity in my goals and the courage to act on them."

Gemini

16-November-2026

The cosmos invites you inward, Gemini, asking you to slow down and reflect. Your inner world needs attention, and rest will help restore balance. Dreams, intuition, or subtle nudges may provide valuable guidance. This is not a day to force progress but to honour stillness and allow clarity to surface naturally. Meditation, journaling, or creative expression will feel especially rewarding. Trust that even in quiet moments, growth is happening. By nurturing your inner world, you prepare yourself for the energy and opportunities soon to come.

Affirmation & Gratitude

"I honour rest and trust the wisdom that arises from stillness."

Gemini

17-November-2026

A wave of fresh energy returns today, Gemini, bringing vitality, confidence, and boldness. This is the perfect time to start a project, showcase your talents, or express your individuality more fully. Others are drawn to your lively energy, and doors may open because of your charm and authenticity. Focus on one inspired direction instead of scattering your attention across many. Progress flows easily when you trust your instincts and act with courage. The stars encourage you to embrace your uniqueness—it's what makes you magnetic and successful.

Affirmation & Gratitude

"I celebrate my individuality and embrace new opportunities with confidence."

Gemini
18-November-2026

Relationships take the spotlight today, Gemini. The stars encourage you to focus on cooperation, compromise, and meaningful exchanges. If you've been avoiding a conversation, now is the time to address it with honesty and patience. Your natural wit and warmth can ease tension, but true harmony requires vulnerability and listening as much as speaking. If single, this could be a day where someone intriguing catches your attention. If partnered, it's a chance to strengthen trust and reaffirm your shared goals. Authentic connection blossoms when you show up fully and truthfully.

Affirmation & Gratitude

"I am grateful for relationships built on honesty, balance, and mutual respect."

Gemini

19-November-2026

Gemini, today highlights practical responsibilities and routines. While your adaptable spirit craves variety, the stars remind you of the importance of structure. Focus on your health, finances, or organisation. Productivity flows best when you simplify your priorities and commit to one task at a time. These small, steady steps create a foundation strong enough to support your bigger dreams. Don't underestimate the power of consistency—it's what turns goals into reality. By tending to the details now, you'll create space for greater creativity and exploration later.

Affirmation & Gratitude

"I am thankful for the steady habits that bring balance and stability to my life."

Gemini

20-November-2026

Adventure energy rises again, Gemini, urging you to stretch beyond your comfort zone. This is a day for exploration, whether through travel, study, or diving into fresh conversations. Don't shy away from perspectives that challenge your own—they may spark growth and new inspiration. Curiosity is your compass, and today it will lead you to discoveries that energise your spirit. By saying yes to new experiences, you'll uncover opportunities that shape your future path in exciting ways. Trust your adaptability—it will carry you through the unknown with ease.

Affirmation & Gratitude

"I welcome new perspectives and the growth they bring into my journey."

Gemini

21-November-2026

Gemini, your career and ambitions take centre stage today. Recognition may come for your hard work, or you may feel motivated to clarify your long-term goals. The stars encourage you to act with strategy and authenticity—aligning your ambitions with your deeper values ensures lasting fulfilment. Authority figures or mentors may offer useful advice, but ultimately, trust your instincts to guide you. Don't spread yourself too thin; choose one path that excites you most. Purposeful, consistent action will carry you far now, bringing you closer to your true vision of success.

Affirmation & Gratitude

"I am grateful for clarity in my ambitions and the courage to act authentically."

Gemini

22-November-2026

The cosmos encourages rest and reflection today. Gemini, after days of outward focus, your spirit needs quiet time to recharge. Pay attention to your dreams, intuition, or subtle nudges—they may hold the answers you've been seeking. Avoid filling your schedule with unnecessary tasks. Instead, embrace stillness, journaling, or creative practices that soothe your soul. Trust that slowing down is not wasted time but a vital part of your progress. Balance comes when you honour both action and rest equally. By pausing now, you prepare yourself for the momentum soon to come.

Affirmation & Gratitude

"I honour rest and reflection as essential for clarity and growth."

Gemini

23-November-2026

Fresh, confident energy returns, Gemini, inspiring boldness and self-expression. This is a great day to launch new ideas, showcase your creativity, or take initiative in areas that excite you. People are drawn to your charm and originality, and opportunities may arise because of your openness. Avoid scattering your focus —choose one inspired direction and commit fully. Authenticity is your superpower now. Trust yourself to act courageously and to step into spaces where you can shine. The universe supports your individuality, reminding you that your uniqueness is your strength.

Affirmation & Gratitude

"I celebrate my individuality and take bold steps toward my dreams."

Gemini

24-November-2026

Relationships come into focus once again, Gemini. Today is about balance, trust, and cooperation. Conversations may carry extra weight, giving you the chance to resolve misunderstandings or deepen bonds. Don't gloss over issues with humour—authenticity and honesty are what nurture connection. If single, you may encounter someone who excites your curiosity. If partnered, this is a beautiful day to renew your commitment and reaffirm your shared values. The stars remind you that relationships flourish when both sides feel heard, seen, and respected equally.

Affirmation & Gratitude

"I am grateful for the love and trust that strengthen my connections."

Gemini
25-November-2026

Gemini, today highlights your routines, health, and responsibilities. While you thrive on change and spontaneity, the stars encourage you to find grounding in structure. Small actions—like tidying your space, reviewing finances, or focusing on self-care—will bring lasting benefits. Productivity flows when you approach tasks one at a time instead of scattering your attention. Think of today as laying bricks in the foundation of your future—simple but powerful. The stability you create now gives you the freedom to explore more later. Balance between routine and adventure ensures harmony in your life.

Affirmation & Gratitude

"I am thankful for the routines that support my balance, health, and growth."

Gemini

26-November-2026

Adventure energy stirs again, Gemini, filling you with curiosity and restlessness. This is the perfect day to step outside your comfort zone, whether through travel, study, or meaningful conversations that inspire you. Don't dismiss opportunities simply because they're unfamiliar—the unknown holds the promise of growth. Your natural adaptability makes you well-prepared to handle whatever arises. Follow your curiosity and let it lead you to discoveries that spark excitement and expansion. Inspiration and renewal await if you say yes to the adventure calling your name today.

Affirmation & Gratitude

"I welcome new perspectives and embrace the wisdom they bring into my journey."

Gemini

27-November-2026

Gemini, career and ambition rise to the forefront today. Recognition may come your way, or you may feel a renewed drive to clarify your long-term vision. Align your goals with your authentic self—success feels most fulfilling when it reflects your true values. Authority figures or mentors could provide helpful guidance, but remember to trust your instincts too. Don't scatter your energy across too many opportunities; focus instead on one meaningful direction. Purposeful, authentic steps will create momentum now, carrying you closer to your aspirations.

Affirmation & Gratitude

"I am grateful for clarity in my goals and the courage to pursue them."

Gemini

28-November-2026

The cosmos turns your focus inward, Gemini, inviting you to rest and reflect. After days of outward action, your spirit craves balance and quiet. Pay attention to your intuition, dreams, or subtle nudges—they may reveal insights you've overlooked. Don't overload your schedule today; instead, carve out space for meditation, journaling, or simply being still. Remember, pausing is not wasted time—it's what allows clarity and inspiration to surface. By honouring your inner world, you prepare yourself for fresh opportunities that align with your highest good.

Affirmation & Gratitude

"I honour rest and trust my inner wisdom to guide me forward."

Gemini
29-November-2026

Fresh energy fills your day, Gemini, boosting confidence, creativity, and motivation. This is the perfect time to showcase your talents, begin a project, or take initiative in areas that inspire you. People are drawn to your lively presence, and opportunities may arise unexpectedly. The stars encourage you to focus your energy instead of scattering it. Choose one inspired pursuit and commit fully. Authenticity will carry you further than imitation—trust your individuality. By leading with courage and joy, you'll create momentum that inspires yourself and others.

Affirmation & Gratitude

"I celebrate my individuality and embrace bold opportunities with joy."

Gemini

30-November-2026

Gemini, relationships are highlighted once more. Balance, compromise, and communication are essential today. Don't gloss over deeper issues—your ability to combine humour with honesty allows you to navigate conversations gracefully. If single, you may feel drawn to someone who sparks your curiosity. If partnered, this is a chance to strengthen bonds by addressing concerns openly and reaffirming trust. Authenticity matters most—showing up fully ensures your connections grow stronger. Remember, true harmony is built on respect, patience, and a willingness to meet in the middle.

Affirmation & Gratitude

"I am grateful for the trust and love that nurture my relationships."

December 2026

Gemini
01-December-2026

Practical responsibilities step into focus today, Gemini. The stars remind you that structure is not a restriction but a foundation for your freedom. This is a good day to organise your space, focus on health routines, or handle important details. Avoid multitasking—choose one priority and complete it fully. Productivity feels satisfying now, and the small steps you take will ripple into lasting benefits. By honouring discipline today, you create balance and stability that support your adventurous side tomorrow. Consistency is the key to long-term growth and ease.

Affirmation & Gratitude

"I am thankful for the steady habits that bring order and balance to my life."

Gemini
02-December-2026

Adventure energy rises strongly today, Gemini, stirring your curiosity and desire to explore. Whether through travel, study, or meaningful conversations, the universe invites you to step beyond your familiar routines. Inspiration may come from unexpected places—a book, a new person, or an idea that challenges your thinking. Don't be afraid of the unknown; your adaptability makes you ready to embrace it with excitement. The cosmos is nudging you to say yes to experiences that broaden your horizons. Growth and renewal await in the new paths you explore today.

Affirmation & Gratitude

"I welcome new experiences and trust the growth they bring into my journey."

Gemini
03-December-2026

Gemini, career and ambitions take the spotlight today. Recognition for your hard work may come your way, or you may feel a push to refine your long-term goals. Align your ambitions with your values to ensure the success you seek feels authentic and fulfilling. A mentor, colleague, or authority figure may offer advice that helps you gain clarity. Don't scatter your focus; concentrate on one path that inspires you most. The stars remind you that confidence and authenticity are your strongest allies for professional growth.

Affirmation & Gratitude

"I am grateful for clarity in my goals and the courage to pursue them."

Gemini
04-December-2026

The cosmos calls you inward, Gemini, encouraging you to pause and reflect. After days of outward momentum, your inner world needs attention. Trust your intuition and pay attention to subtle nudges, dreams, or flashes of insight—they may reveal truths you've overlooked. Avoid overloading yourself with obligations today. Instead, honour rest and allow yourself time to recharge. This is not wasted energy; it's a vital part of your balance. By listening to your inner voice, you'll find clarity and renewal for the opportunities ahead.

Affirmation & Gratitude

"I honour rest and trust my intuition to guide me forward with wisdom."

Gemini
05-December-2026

Fresh energy flows through your day, Gemini, bringing confidence and courage. This is a great time to act boldly, showcase your talents, or begin a project that excites you. People notice your magnetic presence, and opportunities may arise simply because of your authenticity. Avoid scattering your efforts; focus instead on one inspired path and commit to it. The stars support bold, authentic action now. Trust your instincts, and you'll create momentum that carries you forward with joy. Celebrate your individuality—it's your greatest strength.

Affirmation & Gratitude

"I celebrate my uniqueness and step forward with courage and joy."

Gemini

06-December-2026

Gemini, relationships are highlighted once more. Balance, compromise, and authenticity will strengthen your connections today. This is a powerful day for honest conversations—your ability to blend humour with openness makes tough topics easier to approach. If single, you may meet someone through social circles who sparks your interest. If partnered, it's a good time to reaffirm your commitment and work on shared goals. Remember, harmony grows when both sides feel valued and respected equally. Authentic connection always comes from showing up fully as yourself.

Affirmation & Gratitude

"I am grateful for the love, respect, and trust that deepen my relationships."

Gemini
07-December-2026

Practical responsibilities and routines are emphasised today, Gemini. While you may prefer variety, the stars remind you of the grounding power of structure. Focus on organisation, health, or finances. Productivity flows when you simplify and handle one task at a time instead of juggling too much. Even small steps today will ripple into long-term balance and stability. By tending to these details, you create a foundation that supports your adventurous side. Discipline today is an investment in tomorrow's freedom. The cosmos is rewarding steady effort now.

Affirmation & Gratitude

"I am thankful for the routines that bring balance and stability into my life."

Gemini
08-December-2026

Adventure calls again, Gemini, filling you with restlessness and excitement. The universe encourages you to embrace new experiences that stretch your comfort zone. Travel, study, or connecting with inspiring people may bring insights that change how you see your path forward. Don't dismiss opportunities just because they seem unfamiliar—the unknown holds the key to growth. Your natural adaptability makes you ready for change. Say yes to experiences that awaken your curiosity and inspire fresh momentum. Trust your inner compass—it will guide you toward expansion.

Affirmation & Gratitude

"I welcome adventure and embrace the wisdom of new experiences."

Gemini
09-December-2026

Gemini, career and ambitions take centre stage again today. Recognition for your past efforts may appear, or you may feel inspired to set clearer goals for your future. The cosmos encourages you to align your ambitions with your values, ensuring that your definition of success feels authentic. Mentors or authority figures may offer valuable insights, but remember to trust your instincts above all. Avoid scattering your focus—commit to one meaningful direction. Strategic, steady progress is your best path forward now, helping you build momentum that will carry you into the year ahead.

Affirmation & Gratitude

"I am grateful for clarity in my goals and the courage to pursue them."

Gemini
10-December-2026

The cosmos calls you inward today, Gemini. After recent outward focus, your spirit needs stillness and reflection. Dreams, intuition, or quiet nudges may reveal important truths. This is not a day to push ahead with force; instead, step back and allow clarity to rise naturally. Honour your inner world by journaling, meditating, or spending time in solitude. Avoid overloading your schedule, as peace will bring greater insights than activity now. Trust that rest and reflection prepare you for new energy. By slowing down, you create balance between your inner and outer worlds.

Affirmation & Gratitude

"I honour rest and reflection, trusting they restore my clarity and strength."

Gemini
11-December-2026

Fresh, vibrant energy surrounds you today, Gemini, filling you with confidence and creativity. This is an excellent time to take bold action, start a project, or share your ideas with others. Your charm and enthusiasm make you magnetic, drawing opportunities your way. Focus your energy instead of scattering it—choose one inspired pursuit and commit fully. Authenticity is your greatest strength, and the stars are encouraging you to lead with it. By trusting yourself and embracing your individuality, you'll spark progress that inspires you and those around you.

Affirmation & Gratitude

"I celebrate my individuality and embrace new beginnings with confidence."

Gemini
12-December-2026

Relationships come into focus today, Gemini. The cosmos encourages you to seek balance, trust, and cooperation. Don't avoid important discussions—your ability to communicate clearly and warmly can bridge gaps with ease. If single, this is a favourable time to meet someone who excites your curiosity. If partnered, today is an opportunity to strengthen your connection by reaffirming shared goals and trust. Remember, authentic harmony is built on respect, honesty, and patience. When you show up fully and listen as much as you speak, your connections grow stronger and more fulfilling.

Affirmation & Gratitude

"I am grateful for the love, trust, and balance that nurture my relationships."

Gemini

13-December-2026

Gemini, today is about routines, organisation, and responsibilities. While your spirit loves spontaneity, the stars remind you of the grounding power of structure. Tidy your space, handle financial matters, or focus on self-care routines that boost your wellbeing. Productivity flows when you commit to one task at a time instead of scattering your energy. Even small efforts today will ripple into lasting stability. Think of this as maintenance for your life, strengthening the base that supports your bigger dreams. Structure today will give you freedom tomorrow—it's the balance you thrive on.

Affirmation & Gratitude

"I am thankful for the routines that bring order, health, and balance to my life."

Gemini
14-December-2026

Adventure energy calls once more, Gemini, urging you to explore beyond your familiar boundaries. Whether through travel, study, or connecting with inspiring people, you're being invited to expand your horizons. Inspiration may come from unexpected places, sparking new ideas and perspectives. Don't be afraid to step into unfamiliar territory—your adaptability makes you more than capable. The universe is encouraging you to trust your curiosity and follow it boldly. Growth, renewal, and fresh excitement await when you embrace exploration. This is a day for saying yes to discovery.

Affirmation & Gratitude

"I welcome new experiences and the wisdom they bring into my journey."

Gemini

15-December-2026

Gemini, career and ambitions are in the spotlight today. Recognition may arrive, or you may feel inspired to refine your long-term vision. Use this energy to align your goals with your authentic self. Conversations with mentors or colleagues could bring clarity, but ultimately your instincts will guide you best. Avoid scattering your attention—choose one goal and move toward it with confidence. Progress flows when you combine strategy with courage. The stars remind you that success is not about speed but about authenticity and alignment with your values.

Affirmation & Gratitude

"I am grateful for clarity in my ambitions and the courage to act authentically."

Gemini
16-December-2026

The cosmos encourages rest and reflection today, Gemini. After a busy stretch, your inner world needs attention. Don't pressure yourself to perform or produce—give yourself permission to slow down. Pay attention to your intuition, dreams, or synchronicities; they may reveal insights about your next steps. Journaling, meditation, or simply spending time in stillness will be especially healing. Trust that progress is happening even when it looks like stillness. By honouring your inner world today, you prepare yourself for the fresh opportunities and energy that await you tomorrow.

Affirmation & Gratitude

"I honour stillness and trust my intuition to guide me with clarity."

Gemini
17-December-2026

Gemini, vibrant energy returns, boosting your confidence and self-expression. This is a great day to start a new project, embrace creativity, or share your ideas boldly. Your natural wit and adaptability attract people, and opportunities may appear simply because of your authentic energy. Focus on what excites you most instead of scattering your efforts too widely. The universe encourages you to lean into your individuality—it's your superpower. When you act with courage and authenticity, you'll not only inspire yourself but also those who cross your path. Shine brightly today—it's your time.

Affirmation & Gratitude
"I celebrate my individuality and embrace new beginnings with courage."

Gemini
18-December-2026

Relationships are in focus today, Gemini, and the stars highlight balance, compromise, and communication. This is a powerful day to address unresolved issues or to deepen bonds through honest exchanges. Don't gloss over what matters—your gift for words can help bring clarity and ease tension. If single, this could be a day where someone intriguing enters your life. If partnered, it's an opportunity to reaffirm commitment and reconnect. Authentic connection requires honesty, respect, and patience, all of which are within your reach today. Trust your ability to create harmony.

Affirmation & Gratitude
"I am grateful for the trust and love that strengthen my relationships."

Gemini
19-December-2026

Gemini, today is about grounding yourself in routines, health, and practical responsibilities. While your airy energy loves freedom, the cosmos reminds you that structure creates stability. Focus on organisation, tidying, or self-care routines that support your wellbeing. Productivity will flow if you avoid multitasking and take things step by step. Think of today as maintenance work—necessary for building a solid foundation that supports your dreams. By handling details now, you'll free yourself to embrace future adventures with confidence. Balance comes from honouring both routine and spontaneity in equal measure.

Affirmation & Gratitude

"I am thankful for the habits that bring balance, health, and stability."

Gemini
20-December-2026

Adventure stirs your spirit today, Gemini, filling you with curiosity and restlessness. This is an ideal time to explore, whether through travel, study, or connecting with people who inspire new perspectives. Don't hesitate to step into unfamiliar territory—the unknown holds opportunities for growth and renewal. Conversations may spark powerful insights, leading you to ideas that reshape your direction. Your adaptability ensures you can thrive no matter what you encounter. Follow your curiosity, and you'll find excitement and inspiration waiting in unexpected places. Trust the journey—it will enrich your path.

Affirmation & Gratitude

"I welcome new perspectives and embrace the wisdom they bring into my journey."

Gemini

21-December-2026

Career and ambition rise to the surface today, Gemini. Recognition for your work is possible, or you may feel a renewed push to refine your long-term goals. Align your vision with your authentic values to ensure your success feels meaningful. Conversations with mentors or authority figures may offer clarity—stay open to their perspective while trusting your instincts. Avoid scattering your focus across too many directions. When you combine strategic effort with authenticity, you'll create lasting momentum. The stars encourage you to step forward confidently—your unique approach is your greatest strength.

Affirmation & Gratitude

"I am grateful for clarity in my ambitions and the courage to act authentically."

Gemini
22-December-2026

The cosmos calls you inward again, Gemini, reminding you that balance requires moments of stillness. After recent outward focus, today is about pausing to recharge. Trust your intuition—it may reveal subtle insights or guidance about your next steps. Rest, journaling, or meditation will be especially restorative now. Don't overload your day with obligations; instead, create space for peace and reflection. Remember, rest is not wasted time but an essential part of growth. By listening to your inner world, you'll uncover clarity and strength that prepare you for tomorrow's opportunities.

Affirmation & Gratitude

"I honour rest and trust the wisdom it brings into my journey."

Gemini

23-December-2026

Fresh, lively energy flows into your day, Gemini, boosting your confidence and creativity. This is the perfect time to start something new, showcase your talents, or embrace bold self-expression. Others are drawn to your charisma, and opportunities may arise simply because of your openness. Avoid scattering your energy across too many pursuits—focus on one inspired path and give it your full attention. The universe encourages you to act with authenticity and courage. By stepping forward bravely and leaning into your individuality, you'll create momentum that carries you well into the future.

Affirmation & Gratitude

"I celebrate my individuality and embrace opportunities with courage and joy."

Gemini
24-December-2026

Relationships and partnerships come into focus today, Gemini. The cosmos highlights cooperation, balance, and honest exchanges. If single, this could be a day where someone intriguing enters your orbit. If partnered, it's a wonderful time to deepen trust and reaffirm shared values. Don't gloss over important topics—your ability to communicate clearly will strengthen bonds. Authentic connections thrive when both sides feel respected and valued. Use your natural wit and charm to keep conversations light, but remember that depth and truth are equally important. Show up authentically—it will nurture harmony.

Affirmation & Gratitude

"I am grateful for the love, honesty, and balance that strengthen my relationships."

Gemini
25-December-2026

Gemini, today invites you to focus on routines, health, and responsibilities. While the festive energy of the day may tempt you to scatter yourself, the stars remind you that balance matters. Honour your body with rest, good food, and self-care, even as you celebrate. Organisation and small acts of grounding will create a sense of peace amid the bustle. Think of this as tending to your inner wellbeing so you can enjoy the joy of the season more fully. Balance between indulgence and discipline will leave you feeling energised, not drained.

Affirmation & Gratitude

"I am thankful for the balance that supports joy and wellbeing in my life."

Gemini
26-December-2026

Adventure energy stirs again, Gemini, inspiring you to seek out experiences that expand your horizons. This could involve travel, meaningful conversations, or exploring new perspectives. Your curiosity is heightened, and the universe encourages you to follow it boldly. Don't dismiss the unfamiliar—it may hold the inspiration you need. By embracing exploration, you'll uncover insights that reshape your direction. Your adaptability ensures that you thrive in new situations. Say yes to what excites you today; it will bring growth, renewal, and joy to your path forward.

Affirmation & Gratitude

"I welcome new experiences and the growth they bring into my journey."

Gemini
27-December-2026

Gemini, career and ambitions come into sharp focus today. Recognition for your skills may arrive, or you may feel called to refine your long-term goals with greater clarity. The stars remind you to align your ambitions with your authentic values—success is most fulfilling when it feels true to you. Mentors, colleagues, or authority figures may offer valuable advice. Avoid scattering your energy across too many paths; choose the one that excites your spirit most. With strategy and courage, you'll make progress that lasts well into the new year.

Affirmation & Gratitude

"I am grateful for clarity in my ambitions and the courage to pursue them."

Gemini
28-December-2026

The cosmos invites you inward today, Gemini. After recent activity, your spirit needs reflection and renewal. This is not a day to rush or push forward. Instead, carve out time for stillness—journaling, meditation, or quiet self-care will be especially healing. Pay attention to dreams or intuitive nudges; they may reveal insights you've been overlooking. Trust that rest is not wasted time but an essential part of balance. By listening to your inner world, you prepare yourself for the opportunities ahead. Reflection today plants the seeds for clarity tomorrow.

Affirmation & Gratitude

"I honour rest and trust the wisdom my intuition provides."

Gemini
29-December-2026

Fresh energy surges into your day, Gemini, filling you with vitality, creativity, and confidence. This is a great time to embrace bold action, share your ideas, or begin something new. Your charm makes you magnetic, and others may be drawn to your enthusiasm. Avoid scattering your focus—choose one inspired pursuit and commit wholeheartedly. The universe encourages you to lead with authenticity and courage. When you act from your true self, opportunities unfold naturally. Celebrate your uniqueness today; it's your greatest gift and the source of your momentum.

Affirmation & Gratitude

"I celebrate my uniqueness and step into new opportunities with confidence."

Gemini
30-December-2026

Gemini, relationships take the spotlight today. The stars ask you to focus on balance, trust, and cooperation. This is a good time to engage in heartfelt conversations that clear the air and strengthen bonds. If you're single, you may encounter someone intriguing who resonates with your energy. If partnered, this is an opportunity to reaffirm your connection and revisit shared goals. Remember, harmony is not about avoiding differences but about working through them with patience and respect. Authenticity in your words and actions will nurture bonds that stand the test of time.

Affirmation & Gratitude

"I am grateful for the love, honesty, and trust that deepen my connections."

Gemini
31-December-2026

Gemini, as the year draws to a close, the cosmos reminds you to pause and reflect on your journey. Celebrate the progress you've made, no matter how big or small, and acknowledge the lessons that shaped your growth. Avoid rushing into the new year without honouring what you've achieved. This is a powerful day for gratitude and intention-setting. Spend time journaling, meditating, or sharing reflections with those closest to you. By releasing what no longer serves you, you create space for new opportunities in 2027. Balance comes from closure and fresh beginnings.

Affirmation & Gratitude

"I am thankful for the lessons of the past year and welcome new beginnings with an open heart."

www.ingramcontent.com/pod-product-compliance
Lightning Source LLC
Chambersburg PA
CBHW071145070526
44584CB00019B/2669